In at the
Deep End

How a young farmer came to cultivate the media

David Richardson

First published by Poppyland Publishing, Cromer 2016

ISBN 9781912821976

A CIP catalogue record for this book
is available from the British Library

Revised April 13 2021
Published 2021 Tricorn Books
131 High Street, Portsmouth,
PO1 2HW

Printed & bound in the UK

Contents

PREFACE

I have had the great honour of knowing David nearly half my life. He has been my friend, my mentor and confidant. Above all, he has given me the opportunity of pursuing my dream: driving forward more sustainable agriculture and better public engagement in farming, through my role with LEAF (Linking Environment And Farming).

David's book spans over 80 years of an ever-changing farming industry. It is hard to imagine farming without electricity in this country, our dependency on horses for cultivations and the long years of food rations, yet David's journey through an industry so changed is gripping and fascinating. David has taken every opportunity life has thrown at him and grown a remarkable career in journalism alongside a real visionary approach for farming. Indeed, there are few in the farming industry that have not heard of him.

It is clear he has never stopped learning. Always hungry to share his wisdom, experiences, travels, thoughts, grumbles, and joy. Indeed, he stresses so often how pleased he was to be given the opportunity to share his good fortune over his lifetime and put something back into an industry that has given him so much. But it is clear this is not without sheer hard work and commitment backed up by the support of his wonderful wife, Lorna, sadly no longer with us, and his family that has meant that he has constantly given back so much to the industry all his life with time, commitment and through television, radio and his pen.

And all of this with a questioning mind, an open heart, and a sparkle in his eye. How true his quote in this book, 'in my view humour is the oil that makes the mechanics of human relations function. Without it life is

7

dry, boring, less enjoyable and less efficient'.

This book is a truly beautiful account of farming through David's life, with descriptions that take you onto his farm, his intrepid travels, the joys of the Young Farmers Club and the trials and tribulations that life throws at us over the years. During that time there are things that were done differently and that we are sad we have lost, there are new things that have provided opportunities for farmers and indeed the consumers we feed and of course there are those things that have happened before that we still do not learn from.

This book is for everyone, the young farmers stepping up to meet the challenges of playing a part in one of the most important industries in the world; those of us already involved in farming as a reminder of the importance of balancing the lessons of history with more recent developments. It is also for the government and policy makers as a prompt to learn from our experiences, both here in the UK and across the globe, of what really matters: producing food in the most sustainable ways possible in order to secure the health of our precious natural resources and the wellbeing of mankind.

This book is full of life's lessons, underpinned by David's strong moral judgement and belief in fairness, honesty, and integrity.

There are many heroes in farming and then there are legends. Those individuals that stand out. David is a true legend, and I am proud I know him.

Caroline Drummond, MBE
LEAF Chief Executive

FOREWORD
BY LORD PLUMB OF COLESHILL

David always tells it as it is – no if's – no but's. His book is a remarkable story of taking opportunities when facing deep ends. A story of his family as he tells of life as it was, his farming career in Norfolk, the places of interest and events he has attended around the world. He remembers with pride his background, years of struggle and achievement. But above all the support he received from his parents during his early life. They were always ready with advice and encouragement.

His enthusiasm and support for young farmers at club and county level set a fine example for fellow members in Norfolk. This provided him with a springboard to follow the motto "get up, speak up and shut up". His wit and natural charm were infectious, but his firm resolve to speak up for his fellow farmers gave him a platform of opportunity which led to journalism, public debate and broadcasting on radio and TV. Representing his county at County and National meetings was our first brief contact since my role representing Warwickshire as a young farmer was so similar.

He met Lorna when she was secretary of a neighbouring Young Farmers Club as I did my wife, Marjorie. Hence the truism that YFC's are the finest marriage bureau in the country. We have both been fortunate to have their support and regular advice while moving through deep ends so often away from home. We have wonderful families.

David describes his early days when children did what their parents told them. Like when his mother was furious with him for taking money from people on his school bus for playing his euphonium. He could obviously attract an audience early in his life!

His father's advice when he started work was wise and sound. Go and work for someone else before coming back to the home farm, he said, and you will then better understand the importance of relationships between employer and employee. Cycling three miles to milk cows at 4.30 am every morning as a teenager was a test of courage and spirit.

No university, no college, just a wise father and family who encouraged his enthusiasm and work ethic in farming. David learned the subtle difference between being a good farmer and a successful farmer. The

Norfolk four course rotation was his foundation, but he quickly learned that to make a living you also had to diversify and be flexible.

The growth of his farming operation makes fascinating reading both for those who have experienced farming over the years and for young farmers who can learn from the Richardson story as they plan their future.

David's expertise in various media gave him an opportunity to provide facts to his fellow journalists in an easily digested form free from boring statistics and distortion and also to educate consumers as well as farmers. He found inspiration at the annual Oxford Conference attending fifty without a break.

In a speech David made in Memphis, Tennessee, his theme was sustainability in farming long before that was a popular concept. This led to the birth of LEAF, Linking Environment And Farming, which has been a huge success. I pay tribute to him for his initiative in helping to initiate the organisation which has achieved so much. It has, for instance, encouraged more than a million people to visit farms on Open Farm Sunday's.

Many of David's initiatives have not been for personal gain – LEAF being a case in point. And his book is full of basic common sense and proof that his ideas have borne fruit. He was a tough but straightforward interviewer on various radio and TV programmes as I know from experience. He accused me once of being "a bit like a poacher turned gamekeeper who still did some poaching on the side".

He is a good friend who I respect and his record stands alongside many highly respected communicators through the centuries. It is a real privilege to write a Foreword for this book that we should all read.

Henry Plumb

INTRODUCTION

For many years whenever I have met anyone for the first time the conversation soon turns to how and why an ordinary Norfolk farmer like me has spent a good proportion of my life doing things in the media. They always seem interested in what I tell them and that is my excuse for being arrogant and boastful enough to write about my life in the assumption that someone might want to read it.

My stock answer when anyone asks how it happened is "I needed the money" and that, as you will read in the pages that follow, is not entirely facetious. Not that I can claim to have been hard done by in my youth but there was no silver spoon and every penny had to be counted when I rented my first farm.

But I was lucky. I happened to be in the right place at a number of crucial times in my life and all I did was accept the challenges as they came my way. At times I was pushed "in at the deep end" but somehow managed to swim. I was also lucky in my family. My parents encouraged me; my brother, who later became my partner in business, accepted my absences while I was doing other things; and my late wife, Lorna, looked after our children and tolerated my many trips away when I should probably have been at home to share the responsibility. I tried to pay her back for her forbearance by taking her on lots of farm study tours, which she loved, in the years since.

The reason why people are fascinated by those who appear on TV and radio is that they regard it as glamorous. At my level, a long way from show business, that glamour is a bit of an illusion. Yes, I have met politicians and captains of our agricultural industry, travelled to many countries, and learned a lot. But there were never any red carpets or awards ceremonies. Just the satisfaction of being able to inform others who were interested what was going on in the farming world.

And it was a real privilege to visit many farms and talk to those who farmed them. They taught me so much it was at times like the university course I never took. I look back and can identify many decisions taken on the farm at home which were inspired by people I had gone to interview. Many of those individuals became friends as they still are today and that too is a source of enormous pleasure and satisfaction to me.

But when I look back to the beginning of this fascinating and fortunate life I have led, as an eighteen-year-old boy going to Wymondham Young

Farmers Club for the first time I recognise with gratitude that almost everything worthwhile that has happened to me can be credited to Young Farmer's. I made lifelong friends; learned to speak in public; how to run a meeting; how to write articles; and much more. Best of all I met my wife, Lorna, at a Young Farmers meeting and our union, which continued nearly 60 years until she passed away in 2018, produced three children and three grandchildren in whom we both took great pride. And that's my proudest boast of all.

David Richardson
April 2021

Chapter 1

Birthday Surprise

The date was August 31st, 1960. I remember it clearly because it was my 23rd birthday. On the farm we were three quarters through the grain harvest. But it had rained the day before, so we had stopped combining while the crops dried in the sun. In those days we had no other means of drying. The sun was always the cheapest in any case.

The chaps who worked on the farm were out on tractors, cultivating the stubbles of already harvested cornfields, hand-trimming the hedges of those soon to be ploughed and planted with wheat for the following year, filling up time as productively as possible until we could return to the priority job of harvesting.

On a four-acre field at the end of the farm drive my wife, Lorna, was supervising a small group of local women who were hand picking broad beans for human consumption that we had grown on contract for Birds Eye the frozen food company. Each net of bean pods had to be weighed to ensure it contained the correct 28lbs that Birds Eye required, and then recorded so that each woman could be paid for the number of bags she had picked. Beside the weighing scales in his second-hand sit-up-and-beg-pram was our six-month-old son, Andrew, fast asleep most of the time but occasionally needing attention at one end or the other.

Meanwhile, I was in the little barn cement rendering a grain pit we had recently dug. There were single suckled beef calves grazing the water meadows behind the farmyard, the progeny of a small herd of blue-grey cows I had bought at St Boswells market in Scotland the previous year. In a few weeks they would come into the cattle yards to be fed and finished through the winter and I was preparing to mechanize the delivery of some of our homegrown barley into a second-hand roller-crusher I had bought at an auction.

The idea was to tip bags of barley into the below ground pit in the corner of the small barn, then elevate it up into the hopper of the machine through a then new-fangled three-inch auger, or Archimedes screw. This was powered by a small petrol engine and saved a great deal of back breaking lifting by muscle power. My maternal grandfather was a foreman builder and years before he had taught me to lay bricks, level concrete and plaster walls. So, that day I was plastering, or rendering as the cement version is called, the new grain pit. Not a bad way to spend a birthday, or so I thought at the time.

But although I did not realize it my life was about to change.

A dark green Jaguar car pulled up at the gate of the field where Lorna was weighing beans and the driver asked where he could find me. She directed him down the drive to the farmyard and a few moments later I looked up from my trowel through the open barn door and saw the same car sweep into the yard. I knew at once it was too expensive for a salesman. But with my cement in danger of drying I carried on rendering. At least I did until the driver emerged from the car.

He was a shortish, roundish, man with glasses and although I had never met him before I recognized Dick Joice, who had become East Anglia's celebrity farmer as the presenter of Anglia TV's *Farming Diary* programme since the station came on air in 1959 about a year previously. What on earth is he doing here? I wondered. I could only assume he must be lost.

But my curiosity was aroused. And whereas if I had not known who the Jaguar driver was, I might have kept my head down until he went away, I called out to let him know someone was about. "Are you David Richardson", he enquired. I admitted I was and asked if I could help him.

"To be honest I'm not yet sure", he replied. "But have you got time for a few minutes chat?" To which I agreed, so long as he didn't mind if I continued rendering while the cement was still moist.

So, we chatted while I worked. We talked about farming and how long I had been at Whiterails farm. He said he had met my wife on the bean field, and I told him how yields were going. It was all very friendly, and I was puzzled as to where it was all leading.

And then he said, "The fact is I'm looking for a young farmer to do half a dozen weekly spots on a new regional magazine programme called *About Anglia* which I shall be presenting each weekday evening at 6 O'clock". He went on to explain that it would be a bit like an East Anglian version of the *Tonight* programme which Cliff Michelmore was presenting at the time on BBC television.

At the time I knew very little about television. We didn't have a TV set in the house, partly because we couldn't afford one but mainly because we had no mains electricity on which to power one. The power cables hadn't reached Great Melton by 1960. That took a few more years. My only experience from the inside, so to speak, was as a member of an audience for a televised Young Farmers quiz a few months previously. My memory of that occasion was that it was time consuming, boring, labour intensive and that recording a half hour programme had taken all evening.

I had been elected vice chairman of Norfolk Young Farmers County Federation a few months earlier. It meant visiting clubs around the county, chairing the Finance and General Purposes Committee, and being involved in a host of other YFC activities. It was taking me away from the farm more than I should have been even then. And having rented the farm less than two years before, money and time were very tight indeed.

So, without even asking Dick Joice to clarify what it was he might want me to do, I said, "I don't think I'm your man. I have this farm to run, and I really can't spare the time."

But Dick was no fool. He had instinctively summed up the financial situation I was in during our chat and he said, "Anglia TV would pay you, of course".

I had naturally assumed that I would not be paid. After all, the work I had and still was doing for the YFC's was voluntary. It was enormous fun, but it actually cost me money.

"How much would Anglia pay me?" I asked, with renewed interest. "Oh, I should think about seven guineas an item" he replied. "And how long would I need to be away from the farm?" I continued. "Half a day per appearance should do it" said Dick.

Now you need to be aware that my weekly drawings from the farm were £8. Out of that Lorna and I were still paying off a £5 per week hire purchase agreement on the lounge suite. So, my wife, baby son and I were living on £3 a week spending money. If I'm honest, we weren't quite surviving on that meagre sum. My parents were helping and the bright yellow and black ex Wimpey Austin A70 pick-up truck I drove was fuelled by the farm. However, even after that and even back in 1960, £3 a week didn't provide many luxuries.

But what Dick Joice had said led me to the quick realization that seven guineas a week, that's £7.35p in today's money, would more than treble my spending money for the six-week period Dick had mentioned.

"That's different" I said, rather too quickly. "In that case I'll do it."

"Hang on a minute" said Dick "It's not quite as simple as that. We'll have to give you an audition to make sure you look alright on camera".

"Do you have to" I asked," because I have always hated exams and seldom done well at them." I was afraid I might mess up and deny myself that extra spending money.

"Don't worry, you'll sail through" said Dick "I'll phone you in a few days to arrange it". And with that he climbed into his Jaguar and drove out of the yard.

I completed rendering the grain pit in a bit of a daze. I still had no idea why I had been chosen. It suddenly occurred to me that Dick Joice might have several candidates to consider. He must be interviewing any number. All of them probably knew more than I did, and it wouldn't take much for them to be better looking than me. By the time my wife came in from the bean field asking what the visit was all about I had convinced myself that I would never hear from Dick Joice again.

By the end of the third day after his visit there had been no phone call from Anglia TV, and I was even more certain that was the end of the affair. My brief flirtation with fame was clearly over. I told Lorna never to tell a soul that we had been visited by the famous man and resolved to concentrate on farming and forget about a career in the media.

But the following day the call came. It was Dick Joice himself and he invited me to go to Anglia's Norwich studio for an audition a few days later. I stuttered that I would be there and then worried for the whole of the intervening period about what I had let myself in for.

The day of the audition finally dawned. I was in a bit of a state but managed to hide it to all but my wife who I again commanded not to tell anyone because of the probability that I would be rejected. I put on my check sports jacket and cavalry twill trousers, combed back my quiff, and set off in the pick-up for Anglia Television's headquarters in Norwich.

The young ladies who worked at Anglia had always been known for being among the smartest in Norwich, and this was just as true back in the autumn of 1960 as it has continued through the years since. The receptionist who greeted me with modulated tones and wearing the latest fashion to complement her perfect figure was one of the smartest, and I felt like a country bumpkin as I approached her desk.

But at least the area, in the centre of Norwich, where the headquarters was located was familiar. For Anglia, under its first chairman, Lord

George Townshend, had bought and converted the old Agricultural Hall built in 1882 by Norfolk farmers for agricultural exhibitions and livestock shows. It was next to Norwich cattle market where, with my father, I had spent almost every Saturday morning since childhood. The market was moving to its smart new site on the outskirts of Norwich during that same year of 1960.

After checking and ticking my name on a list labelled "Auditions" the receptionist politely led me to The Green Room. Not being familiar with "show business" I only realized sometime later that every television and radio station has a Green Room in which artists wait their turn to perform. What puzzled and worried me was that there were several others sitting uneasily on the easy chairs.

The atmosphere was a bit like a dentist's waiting room. For everyone was clearly pretending to read a magazine while surreptitiously summing up everyone else. I didn't recognize any of them, and to be honest none of them looked like farmers. But my paranoia convinced me they were all there to be auditioned for the same job as myself.

One by one they were led out to some other part of the building and none of them returned. Eventually only myself and one other man remained. So I plucked up courage to ask whether he was there for the farming job. "Gracious, no," he said, "I'm hoping to help the company with its religious programmes". Which at least made me relax a bit? For I might not have as much competition as I had first thought. Incidentally, much later I realized my "religious" colleague in that Green Room was Sidney Carter. He was the man who, among other religious writings, wrote modern words to an old Shaker hymn, known better today as *Lord of the Dance*.

Eventually it was my turn. Another of Anglia's pretty ladies collected me and took me along a passage and through two rubber-rimmed doors that made sucking noises as they were opened and closed. It was rather like an airlock and was, I found out later, for soundproofing. Then into a large and rather dark room at the far end of which was a brightly lit area where there were two comfortable looking chairs. Dick Joice was sitting in one of them.

"Hello David" he called, as if we were old friends, "Sorry to keep you waiting. Come and sit down."

Still wondering what was going on but made to feel much more comfortable by Dick's friendly greeting I walked over and sat in the second chair. And Dick immediately began asking me about the farm. Had I finished rendering the grain pit? How was harvest going? Had crops been good this year? Did the sugar beet look promising? And so on.

I quickly became totally relaxed. For these were matters I knew about and was involved with every day. I don't know how long the conversation lasted but we must have been talking for several minutes when Dick said "I reckon that'll do David. I'll give you a ring and let you know what we decide".

I was clearly being dismissed. "But what about the audition?" I asked.

"Blarst boy you've just had it" said Dick laughing. "Off you go and I'll ring you tomorrow".

It must seem pretty stupid in the 21st Century to admit that in 1960 I had not been fully conscious of the fact that I had been ushered into a studio and that I had sat down next to Dick Joice in what TV people call a set. But although I suppose I must have been aware of other people moving about and of big bits of machinery on wheels (TV camera's) in the gloom around us, I had no idea while it was happening that my conversation with Dick was an audition.

It helped that in those early days videotape had not been invented. If it had the whole thing would have been recorded for later viewing by all sorts of people and the tape would have been both caption and voice identified by the studio floor manager as "Audition: David Richardson", together with the date of the recording. The tape would have been allowed to run up to speed and there would have been a verbal and finger countdown from ten seconds before Dick Joice was cued to begin the interview.

But there was none of that. In those days anyone who wanted to know what a potential presenter looked and sounded like on tele had to view him or her live from the gallery above the studio from which everything on the floor was controlled. So, partly by luck and partly because of the skill and sensitivity of Dick Joice, I had just had an audition, or examination, which I had dreaded, without knowing it. And, of course, I had been natural and unselfconscious.

The following day Dick telephoned again and asked when I could start. I was a young working farmer who had left grammar school after doing a mediocre GCSE before I was 16 to work on a neighbour's farm. I had just taken a tenanted farm. I had a young wife and a baby boy and we were living pretty close to the bread line. I knew I was about to be pushed in at the deep end. I hoped I would be able to swim. Little did I know that this was the beginning of an entirely new dimension to my life that would last for well over thirty years.

Chapter 2

In the beginning…

The spring and early summer of 1937 was, I have been assured, rather warm. My father was working with a young lad he employed on a casual basis "scoring up" sugar beet. This is an arduous back breaking task that chemical weed control has since made unnecessary. But in those days, it meant walking through the already hand singled crop in early June to hand hoe out weeds that had grown since "chopping out". This was another manual job that used to be necessary, usually in early May, to leave the single sugar beet plants necessary for an economic crop from the bunch that used to emerge from each natural multi-germ sugar beet seed. These days we plant mono-germ varieties that produce single plants where they are planted. These have been developed and improved by plant breeders since the 1960's.

The lad father was hoeing with was a good worker, although mentally a few bricks short of a load. But he was sharp enough to realize that my mother was pregnant. As he and my father hoed their way along the rows of beet on one of the hottest days of the year he said "I s'pose we shall soon have another young guvnor". Father smiled and said yes, in a couple of months or so. They hoed along the row for a few more yards and the lad continued, "That must be wholly hot in there". To which father said he smiled but did not reply. Then after a pause, "Still, I don't s'pose he care a bugger – he's a ridin".

I was eventually born at the end of August in a Norwich nursing home. Apparently, I was rather a large baby, weighing in at over 10lbs. I was also quite beautiful with lovely curly hair and won prizes at several local baby shows. What a pity that didn't last!

My mother, Hilda, was youngest of the five daughters and one son of Rose and Fred Bowhill of Great Melton in Norfolk. Granny Bowhill had managed to mother this large family in spite of being crippled in mid-life by what must have been polio or something similar. One of my earliest memories is of her sitting, almost permanently, in her chair in the corner of their little living room. Occasionally, when I was very young, she would shuffle across the room to do something in the kitchen using a highchair as a forerunner to a Zimmer frame. But as she grew older her legs would not support her at all and she could only be moved from chair to bed and back in a wheelchair.

Looking back, it is clear that this severe disability must have caused enormous stress on my Grandmother, Grandfather, and the rest of the family. But everybody involved seemed to accept the problem for what it was in a matter-of-fact way and just dealt with it. It certainly didn't spoil the fun I had with my grandparents when, as a small boy, I often pleaded to be allowed to stay with them on Saturday nights when my parents would sometimes go to the "pictures" or the Theatre Royal in Norwich where repertory companies would often perform. I, for my part was allowed to sit up late and listen to the regular Saturday evening Music Hall on the BBC's Home Service. It was the comedians, like Vic Oliver, Tommy Handley, and Rob Wilton that I enjoyed most.

My grandfather, Fred Bowhill, had been a foreman builder supervising construction all over Norfolk. He would walk to the job in hand in the early hours of Monday mornings, supervise the work all week and lodge in a nearby pub, then walk home on Saturday evenings. They worked six-day weeks in those days. As a foreman he was entitled to wear a bowler hat to signify his position – a practice he continued throughout his retirement, which was when I first knew him, and until he died aged 86.

He too was crippled, although less seriously than my grandmother. But he always walked with a stick to help ease his gammy foot. I never did find out the truth of what had caused it but the suspicion was that he had dropped something heavy on it in his youth, breaking some bones, and that they had healed in such a way as to make him lame. He also had several fingers permanently bent, the result, he said, of having handled bricks and cement all his life, but more likely a problem with the tendons in his hands. But physical defects caused by disease or employment were commonplace at the time and they never complained.

My father was the eldest of three children, including two sisters of Edward and Maria Richardson of Hethersett in Norfolk – the next village to Great Melton. Edward Richardson was a small farmer in the village; his wife, my paternal grandmother, who died before I was born, was a talented musician and singer. Both were stalwarts of the Methodist Church just across the road from their little holding called Chapel Farm. My father inherited the farm, all twelve acres of it, and it was my address too for my first twenty-two years.

21

Father and mother met at the Methodist Chapel to which Fred Bowhill would bring his entire family, including his wife, pushed the one and a half miles from Great Melton in a wheelchair, every Sunday.

Grandfather Richardson, who died when I was about three, had been the key-holder of the old Primitive Methodist Chapel in the village, the forerunner of the present Methodist Church. From what evidence I have gleaned his wife was almost certainly the dominant partner, and she was one of the leading lights in the congregation.

My parents followed their religious lead and Methodism was the template around which my early life was formed. My father became a local preacher and travelled around the county to take services. His fine bass voice made him a popular draw and he was often persuaded to sing a solo during his services. My mother had no inclination to perform. In fact, she would have run a mile to avoid it. But she did an enormous amount of good work behind the scenes and there were many in and around Hethersett who benefited from her modest and unobtrusive kindness. There wasn't a lot of money around in my childhood, but there was a lot of love and commitment to the causes in which my family believed.

My earliest memory is of riding on a donkey on Great Yarmouth beach. I could barely have been two years old, because World War II broke out on Sept 3rd, 1939, only a few days after my second birthday. Soon after that the beach was closed off with rolls of barbed wire intended to thwart possible invaders.

Not that my parents had much time or money to take me to Yarmouth. But father used to hire marshes between Acle and Yarmouth each year to provide summer grazing for replacement heifers for the dairy herd we had at the time. Marshmen were employed to look at the cattle daily, but most owners, my father included, liked to visit their animals at least once a fortnight through the summer. It was only a short trip on a Saturday afternoon from the marsh to Yarmouth beach.

Taking small parcels of land wherever he could rent them was how my father started farming. It was hard work and often economically questionable, but he was determined to farm and without adequate capital that was the only way he could do it.

His mother had determined because of the hard times she and my grandfather had had that he should not go into farming at all. He had attended the City of Norwich Grammar School (where I went nearly forty years later) and passed his School Certificate. That meant, in his mother's opinion, that he was well suited for life in an office, and she managed to get him articled as a clerk in a solicitor's office in the middle of Norwich.

To begin with he was little better than the tea boy, but when his employers realized he had copper plate handwriting he was put to copying wills on velum. If typewriters had been invented, they were not used in that office and father tells how he would be paid 6d a page. If he made a mistake, or spelled a word wrongly, he had to pay for a new page of velum himself and rewrite it for nothing. It was hardly surprising he was a stickler for correct spelling and grammar until his dying day.

But he was never happy in an office and he had not been there long before he persuaded his boss to let him have part of Saturday mornings off so he could walk across the road to the livestock market. Before long he was doing a bit of dealing and found he could often earn more at the market on a Saturday morning than the 18 shillings he was being paid for the rest of the week.

He was pondering this one morning as he bicycled from Hethersett to his Norwich office. The bike had been used by a policeman on the beat many years before and was showing its age. The other complication was that he had developed a boil on a particularly sensitive part of his backside. As he urged his bike up Cringleford hill on the outskirts of Norwich, standing on his pedals to do so, the chain broke, letting him down rather suddenly onto the bicycle seat. Needless to say the boil was trapped between backside and seat. He always claimed that was the precise moment he decided to resign from the law. I suspect he may have used a little poetic license to colour the story. But resign he did and to his mother's disgust set out to try to become a farmer.

But he could not have chosen a worse time. The great depression was about to start. None of the marketing boards had been initiated. Prices of farm commodities were falling. But he worked incredibly hard and put together a bunch of scattered fields, a small herd of motley dairy cows and the beginnings of the pig business that was to save his bacon more than once over the coming years.

In between, he courted my mother, got married and they had me. Having left her job working in a haberdasher's shop in Norwich my mother set to work to help on the farm. She hand-churned butter from the milk they were unable to sell to local deliverymen – there was no guaranteed market – and in the absence of a refrigerator hung it down the well until she could take it by bus or bicycle to sell at Wymondham market, three miles away, the following Friday. She sold eggs there too as well as at the door.

It must have been a life of endless toil for her and my father and it went on for several years and until after I was born. There is a family story that I cannot vouch for but which I have been assured is true. Apparently, I was a good child and would sometimes be left in my pram for hours at a time without much attention apart from someone listening in case I cried. On one occasion, the story goes, I was left in my pram at one end of the cowshed. The cowman was asked to listen out for me while mother went off about her other tasks.

Eventually she went back to the cowshed to collect me only to find that I had soiled my nappy and even worse, had kicked it off and smothered myself in its contents. Mother, apparently, threw up her hands in horror and to no-one in particular asked "Whatever shall I do with him?" The cowman, arriving on the scene at the same moment suggested "If he wus mine I'd hull him into a bunch of straw and let him jam it up".

But as the 30's wore on and War looked more likely farmer's incomes including that of my parents began to look up. The Milk Marketing Board had been set up, revolutionizing milk sales and stabilizing prices. Other marketing boards for a number of other commodities followed. The British Sugar Corporation 37% of which had been taken over by the government was looking for sugar beet growers. Agricultural depression faded and prosperity began to seem possible. And father had managed to rent a 137-acre farm in his own village of Hethersett. Prospects were beginning to improve.

Chapter 3

World War II

I cannot claim to remember the outbreak of the 2nd World War. But I can remember sharing the relief of the Nation at the end of it and some of the events in between.

Soon after the war began my father decided to make a bomb shelter. I can only surmise he reasoned that a bomb would only explode if it landed on hard ground and that if the impact could be cushioned the bomb would bounce harmlessly. Why else would he have created a shelter in a flammable haystack?

I feel sure he meant well when he turned a steel cattle trough on its side and then stacked hay deeply over and around it, leaving a small opening at the front so the family could crawl in during an air raid. An old mattress was laid on the floor so we could rest as well as shelter. Hay, of course, has well known insulating properties and the shelter was certainly warm on the coldest nights. I am just grateful the Luftwaffe did not pick us out as a target while we were under the hay.

But the shelter did not last long. Because one night as enemy aircraft droned overhead and we tried to doze in our shelter, a mouse, which also appreciated the warmth, ran past my mother's nose. Ignoring the danger, she screamed and ran outside dragging me with her. She would rather have faced the entire German air force than risk going back into that shelter. At which father just laughed, admitted the haystack was probably a silly idea, and suggested we use the cupboard under the stairs for any future emergencies.

In practice, when, as they often did, raids came at night, he took to standing outside the house watching enemy aircraft as they flew overhead. Usually, they were on their way to a target bigger than Hethersett, but they tended to fly high over Norfolk to get to and from places like Coventry. Except one night, while he was standing outside by the front door watching the action, a stray bomb dropped a hundred yards away on our back field and a piece of red-hot shrapnel from it hit the wall of the farmhouse about eighteen inches from his head. He kept that lump of twisted metal for years as a keepsake. And he stopped standing outside during air raids.

But it wasn't just enemy aircraft that created danger. One morning, father and a bunch of men who worked for and with him by that time, were once again working on the back field. Overhead they heard a low flying aircraft heading straight for them. They noted it was a US Air Force bomber. Looking more carefully they saw its bomb doors were wide open. Further, that the aircraft appeared to be dipping first one wing then the other. Moments later they realized why. A bomb was stuck in its bomb doors and the pilot was attempting to shake it free before landing at one of the many US Air force bases which had, by then, been built in Norfolk. Suddenly they saw the bomb dropping from the plane over the edge of the village.

Instinctively all the men threw themselves flat as the bomb hit the ground and exploded. Shrapnel flew over their prostrate bodies and they were not hurt. Thankfully, nobody else in the village was injured either. Although a young mother pushing her baby in a pram down the village main street was horrified when a piece of shrapnel ripped through both sides of the hood of the pram. Luckily, the baby was lying down. If it had been sitting up the projectile would have gone through its head.

One of my clearest War memories was when Norwich was bombed for the first time. It was on a clear night at the end of April 1942. And although still not five years old even I was allowed outside at midnight to look at the red sky stained with black smoke as Norwich burned six miles to the east. We had no idea whether any of our friends and relations in Norwich had been hit. The next night German bombers came again and there was a repeat performance.

The attacks on Norwich and other well-known cities became known as the Baedeker raids because Adolf Hitler was said to have chosen where to drop his bombs from Baedeker travel guides. Apparently, he wanted to destroy cities with historic buildings of architectural importance. Presumably he thought this would destroy morale. We learned later that during the two raids on Norwich 231 people were killed and 689 injured.

All we could do was watch in helpless awestruck horror from our dark village, there were no streetlights in Hethersett then, as the bombs dropped, and the flames lit up the sky. April 29th was a bright clear night. A fresh wind blew from the east. Next morning when the sun rose there were thousands of pieces of scorched paper blowing around our farmyard. It was even possible to decipher the remains of letterheads on some of them. Norwich businesses as well as dwellings had taken direct hits. The scars left on the Norwich streetscape by that night were to last for many years. There were gaps like lost teeth in some streets; there were deep holes in the ground where major stores had stood; there were distraught families whose loved ones had been among the casualties. I was only a small child, but I remember feeling fortunate to live on a farm in the countryside.

We were fortunate in other ways too. We had ready supplies of milk, eggs and bacon produced on the farm. Although getting enough animal feed coupons entitling my father to buy rations for the cows, chickens and pigs was a frequent problem. Every gallon of milk, every egg and every pig was needed for the War effort. There was a ready market at profitable prices for anything farmers could produce, and the local "War Ag" Committee kept an eye on what every farmer was doing in order to ensure they maximized production. Meanwhile checks were made to ensure they did not cash in on the inevitable black market for food.

One day at the height of the War when, German U Boats were blowing our merchant ships out of the water and Britain almost ran out of food, my mother had a visitor. A sad looking, poorly dressed woman who she had never seen before knocked at the farmhouse door. Mother answered it and asked what she could do for the visitor. At which point the woman launched into a dreadful hard luck story about her mother who she said was desperately ill. The doctor had told her, she claimed, that her mother must have fresh eggs urgently to stay alive and she had no more coupons in her ration book. Please could my mother sell her a dozen eggs? She would pay whatever my mother asked.

Nobody was more soft-hearted than my mother and she would have given her last crust if she had believed the story. But she smelled a rat. She apologized profusely and told the caller that sorry as she was for her mother, she was not allowed to sell eggs outside official channels. The woman began to sob and pleaded with her. But uncharacteristically mother continued to refuse. Afterwards she felt dreadful and almost wished she had given in. At least she did until she heard that two other farmer's wives in the village were being prosecuted for selling eggs illegally. The same woman had visited every farm in the district with her sob story and some had fallen for it. There were dirty tricks as well as heroism during the War.

Some foods we could not get, of course. I well remember, towards the end of the War, as I became old enough to read the Beano and Dandy comics, asking my mother to explain one of the comic strips. Desperate Dan, Korky Cat or some other character in the comic, slipped over on something called a banana skin. "What's a banana?" I asked. Moreover, it took a few years of rationing and food shortages even after the War was over before I actually saw and tasted one.

The greatest danger I faced during the War was on the farm. As a small boy I always spent as much time with my father as possible, even to the extent sometimes of riding with him on his old Standard Fordson while he was ploughing. There was no cab, either for safety or weatherproofing. We just wrapped up in old comb (16 to 18 stone capacity) corn sacks held together with binder twine and took whatever weather arrived. A child riding on such a tractor would be illegal these days but I loved it and never came to grief.

My narrow escape involved a skittish bay gelding carthorse, named Punch. I had gone, aged about four, with my father to the harvest field riding in the back of a horse drawn tumbril fitted with "ladders". These ladders which slotted into brackets on the sides of the tumbril extended the front of the conveyance over the back of the horse and gave similar extra scope at the back. It enabled a tumbril to carry twice as much as it normally would, but sheaves were light compared with, say, a load of sugar beet, so it was a useful way to maximize capacity. In a way it converted a tumbril into a sort of poor man's wagon.

Father had left Punch, with me in the tumbril behind, on the edge of the harvest field and gone to speak to some of his men who were already pitching sheaves and stacking them. At precisely the wrong moment a salesman who was looking for my father drove down the farm road. Punch, who was a marvellous pulling horse but rather nervous, was frightened by the noise of the car and took off across the field, heading for the gate and the farm track beyond, with me bumping about in the tumbril behind him.

Everyone on the field began chasing the runaway, including the salesman into whose car father jumped. In retrospect the noise of the chasing mob probably made Punch even more nervous. But what else could they do? And even when they caught up with the fleeing horse all father could do was lean out of the window shouting for me to keep my head down. For the extension ladders were by this time shaking out of their sockets. The lane down which Punch was now galloping was narrow and there were several trees in the hedgerow.

It was just as well I took my father's advice because it wasn't long before the front ladder, shaken sideways by the vibration of the chase, hit a tree and smashed to smithereens as it passed inches over my head. The rear ladder fell out too somewhere along the road but that was less dangerous for me than for the car that was following which had to stop and move it off the road. Meanwhile Punch and I continued through the village scattering all before us.

By this time we had almost reached the main A11 – the trunk road from Norwich to London. Even in those days it was busy and needed to be approached with care. But Punch did not understand road signs. He just kept galloping straight on, across the traffic, and towards Hethersett station. Fortunately, as he did so, he passed the village policeman's house. Even more fortunately, the officer was at home in his garden. He jumped on his bike and gave chase.

By this time Punch was becoming tired and Hethersett Station Lane is rather hilly. Halfway up the second hill the policeman caught and passed the tumbril and was able to grab the horses bridle and bring him to a halt. Seconds later my father, with his salesman chauffeur arrived on the scene and father almost kissed the policeman. I was lifted out of the back of the cart complaining of a bruised bum, but I was otherwise unharmed. And the salesman offered to take me home to the safety of our farmhouse while father got Punch back to his stable. It was only years later that I fully appreciated what might have happened that day.

I started school soon after that incident. In the village at the time there was the National School that catered mainly for Church of England children and the British School that was mainly for non-conformists, like we Methodists. So, that's where I went. Both schools taught the same things in the same way, as far as I know. It was just a hangover from the days when the churches of various denominations were the main providers of education.

I was never particularly bright, and this was not helped by the fact that I suffered with childhood bronchitis. It was long before antibiotics that would control such problems had been discovered and I was often away from school for several days at a time. During those long days I became an avid reader. I devoured books like Robinson Crusoe, The Swiss Family Robinson, Black Beauty and the like and then moved on to a host of Biggles stories. Any facility I may now have with words may possibly be traced back to all that early reading.

My father loved language as well and Prime Minister Churchill was a wonderful exponent of English. Whenever he broadcast to the nation our little family would gather round the wireless to listen. The message was always important, of course, even if I failed to understand its full significance. But, as a public speaker himself, father was always impressed by the way Churchill expressed himself. We've heard recordings of those speeches repeated many times since, but they never sound as dramatic now as they did when we heard them the first time while "our boys" were out there fighting and enemy aircraft were bombing our land. His words engendered a real sense of national unity, of and pride in adversity and somehow made the privations of war worthwhile.

At school we tried to do our bit to help the troops. Aged about six, along with the rest of the pupils, I was taught to knit. Using recycled wool, pulled out from discarded garments collected from around the village, we knitted scarves for soldiers. Whether they were ever worn I have no idea but knitting them made us feel part of the War effort. Britons have never been as proud of their country since.

There were constant messages on the wireless about "waste not want not". The radio doctor told us how to "keep our bowels regular" on restricted diets. And there were posters in public places declaring "Walls have ears". I didn't know what this meant so I asked my father who explained that we should not talk to strangers because they might be enemy spies. I remember I became obsessed with this concept. For months after acquiring my new knowledge of espionage I regarded every stranger in the village as a suspect. I constantly whispered to my mother and father whenever I saw someone I took to be suspicious and asked if they thought the stranger was a German spy. I remember being quite worried for a while. Perhaps that experience was the root of my lifetime enjoyment of spy novels.

One of the big houses in the village, the Old Hall, was requisitioned by the US air force for its flight crews and officers. I don't remember which airfields they flew from but after the War it became known that the Squadron Leader at Hethel, just a couple of villages away, and later Tibbenham, had been James Stewart who later became a famous film star.

Some of the American servicemen began attending the Methodist Church and my parents befriended them. Several of them were "farm boys" back home and welcomed the opportunity to spend some of their off-duty time in our house. Fortunately, there was food enough from the farm to entertain them and we had some happy and memorable times. One of my favourite Americans was called Dana Andrews and one day he brought round the contents of a food parcel he had just received from home to give to my mother in gratitude for what she had fed him.

There was a bag of yellow grain in the parcel and mother asked what it was. "Why that's corn" said Dana "for making popcorn". None of us knew how to make it so Dana borrowed one of mother's saucepans, took over the cooker, grabbed some highly prized sugar, and showed us how. I can still hear those maize corn grains hitting the underside of the saucepan lid. And I can still remember my first taste of delicious American popcorn.

Meanwhile, my father joined Dad's Army. It was called the Home Guard at the time, but the hilarious television series, which was far more true to life than may now seem likely, adopted a much more appropriate title.

The local squad was ordered to guard an aviation fuel dump beside Hethersett station. Night after night my father and a bunch of mainly middle-aged villagers would sit in the station in case German paratroopers attacked it. Most of their experiences were farcical, but they had a few nasty moments. Like the autumn night they saw lights flashing across a meadow beside the station. A group of them crept along behind the hedges, rifles at the ready, until their commanding officer, an ageing ex-army colonel, came close enough to challenge whoever was out there.

"Halt, who goes there?" he bellowed. "Friend or foe?" Adding for good measure "Drop your weapons and put up your hands". Whether German paratroopers would have understood those questions and commands I don't know. But the shaky reply that came back in broad Norfolk dialect was "Don't shoot, we're only gathering mushrooms".

Chapter 4

Schooldays

The British School at Hethersett seemed enormous to me as a five-year-old. Since then, it has been sold and converted into the Church Hall. But when it was a school the "big room" was divided into three classes by curtains. The fact that both pupils and teachers could hear what was going on in the neighbouring class was at times inconvenient but, like many other things in those wartime days, was accepted as a fact of life that had to be tolerated.

The school was presided over by a fearsome headmistress called Mrs. Maland. She was a large lady with a figure like a ship in full sail, with grey hair swept up into a bun at the back of her head. She wore severe dark dresses buttoned up to the neck and heavy spectacles on the end of her nose. Her reputation was as a disciplinarian and although I never saw it used, it was said she kept a mop handle in her desk to cane naughty boys and girls across the knuckles. Whether it was myth or reality, this weapon, the like of which would be outlawed in the 21st century, had the effect of controlling the behaviour of some pretty tough village characters. Perhaps the threat of capital punishment works as well as the punishment itself.

By the time I was elevated to the "big room" Mrs. Maland had retired and taken her mop handle, if it existed, with her. And Mrs. Batchelor replaced her as headmistress. She was much younger and had a more modern approach as I discovered the day I inadvertently kicked a football in the playground that went through the window behind her desk. My punishment was to clean up the mess, write out a few hundred lines and then pay for the repair in instalment's out of my pocket money.

But I first went to the school, aged five, and joined the infant class run by Miss Curson whose brother was the local builder and funeral director. Classes were in a small room off to the side of the main school. In winter it was heated by a cast iron coke fired burner with the legend "slow but sure" engraved on its decorated surface. That old fire constantly smoked and looking back I would not be at all surprised if the fumes from it made my youthful bronchitis worse. But the seeds of knowledge were sown in my brain in that room, so I remain grateful to it and to those who planted them.

I enjoyed infant school but was always keen to get back to the farm when lessons were over. My maternal grandfather, who had retired from building by this time, spent most of his days pottering around the farm, doing little building jobs for my father, tidying the garden for my mother, and generally making himself useful. One afternoon when I came home from school, I found him beside the hand turned stone grinder we used to sharpen scythe blades, gutting and skinning a rabbit that father had shot somewhere on the farm. We ate rabbit a lot in those days before myxomatosis and this one, like many more before and after was intended for the pot.

Anxious to watch what the old man was doing on the little bench beside the grinder I tried to climb up beside him. The most convenient thing to climb on was the swinging handle of the grinder. But my climb did not last long. As grandfather shouted to tell me to be careful the grinder wheel turned, and I fell awkwardly onto the paving slabs that had been laid beneath to provide a hard base to stand on while sharpening tools. My young bones were soft, and I broke my right forearm in two places.

There followed yet another absence from school while my arm healed inside a plaster cast, during much of which I was able to wander round the farm behind my father. Eventually the day came for the plaster to be cut off. My mother took me to the hospital and back on the bus and when we got home there was a present for me for being a "brave boy". It was a blackboard and easel together with lots of chalk. There weren't too many presents around in those days, so I was ridiculously pleased. Indeed, I would happily have broken the other arm if such rewards were to be standard.

My birthday, August 31st, was the very last day of Norfolk's administrative school year. If I had been born a day later my eligibility to take the 11+ would have been delayed for twelve months. As it was, I sat the exam when I was ten. Surprisingly, I passed and was offered a place at the City of Norwich Grammar School for boys – where my father had gone many years before. Needless to say, father was pleased and the offer was accepted.

The first day was a real shock. The bus ride into Norwich, the size of the school buildings, the mass of pupils, were all intimidating compared with what I had been used to. Back in the village even aged ten I had been a pretty big fish in a very small pool. But at the CNS I was nobody. There I was in my smart new blazer, that was slightly too big for me to allow for growth, the only boy from my school which had a total of about thirty children, suddenly thrown into a single class of thirty-one within a school of 850 mainly city boys.

I knew nobody. There were sixth formers aged up to 18 who seemed like men and prefects who behaved like gods. And the masters all wore gowns. I had never seen the like before and it took me a while to settle in. Truth be told I seldom felt totally comfortable even after five years at the school.

The main exception was the hobbies period that was always the last session on Friday afternoons. There were stamp collectors, amateur radio hams, Esperanto speakers, and so on. But I joined the school young farmers club, which, by definition, had few members. The only prize I ever won at school was for what I did in that club.

But there were some highlights that I remember fondly to this day. The music master, Maurice Doe, and one of the geography masters, Alec Court, decided to put on a production of the Gilbert & Sullivan light opera *The Mikado*, with boys taking all the parts – including the female ones. Mr. Doe was something of a martinet, but an excellent teacher for all that. But Mr. Court was a frustrated actor and while Doe supervised the singing Court did the producing. Together they made an effective team.

I have never had a quality singing voice in spite of my paternal ancestry. But I did, and still do, love all kinds of music, and could carry a tune reasonably well. Aged twelve my treble was not quite high enough for a soprano part. But although my voice was close to breaking it was still high enough for the alto parts and I have always been able to harmonise. So, I found myself cast as one of the chorus of Japanese ladies, wearing a black wig, clad in a geisha girls dress and waving a fan. My classmates and I supported Derek, playing Yum Yum, Tony playing Pitti Sing, and one other whose name escapes me - the "Three little girls from school", and serenaded the sixth formers playing the Emperor and the Lord High Executioner.

We played to packed houses of parents and others in the school hall. We had a lot of fun and learned about much more than singing. We learned about working together across the age groups, about the need to compromise sometimes, about the pleasure to be had from achieving something worthwhile.

With encouragement from my father, who had played in a brass band in his youth, I extended my musical activity after that and began to learn the tenor horn and later the euphonium. I reached the stage where I could play several pieces; most of them hymn tunes which are particularly well suited to the euphonium. My lessons were after normal school time on Friday's, so, carrying my instrument I had to catch a later bus than usual back to the village.

I knew some of the men who always travelled on that later bus. They were builders and other tradesmen who lived in Hethersett and worked in Norwich. "What ha' you got in that cearse Dearvud?" one of them asked me one evening. "Th'as my euphonium" I replied. "Wha's a euphonium when tha's at hum then?" he continued. "Tha's what I play in the school band" I said. "Are yer goin' ter give us a tune then?" he asked. "I don't know about that" I said diffidently. "Go on boy, less hair what you cin do".

So, I got out my instrument and played a couple of hymns to the upper deck of the bus. "Good boy" said my sponsor. "Now then you lot" to the rest of the bus "I'm goin' ter send my hat round fer young Dearvud hair an' I want you to put suffin in it fer the boy". And five minutes later I was handed the results of the collection. As I remember it I received about two shillings, which almost doubled my pocket money of half a crown at the time.

The next week the same thing happened. I played a few hymns, and the hat went round. Before long it was a regular occurrence, and I was beginning to appreciate the rewards of performing. Then one day, one of the bus passengers met my mother in the village shop. "We do enjoy your son's hymns on the bus from Norwich" she told her. Mother knew nothing about it because I had not told her and was nonplussed. She asked her informant what she meant and was told the whole story. But mother was not amused.

That night she told me I should not be playing for money. She said it was almost like begging and a Richardson should be above that sort of thing. And what, in any case, did I think I was doing playing hymns on the top of a bus? I was never to do such a thing again.

In those days children did what their parents told them, and I stopped my top deck recitals as instructed. But while in retrospect I can understand mothers' point of view, the fact is I lost interest in playing soon after that and I suspect I might not have if the profit element had still been there. I have threatened many times to re-learn the euphonium, a lovely mellow instrument, but have never got round to it. Perhaps it's something I will do if and when I retire.

The other thing I enjoyed at school was playing hockey. Always somewhat overweight I was never athletic. Indeed, I dreaded cross-country runs which had to be done but which I thought of as torture. I tried football and rugby without much success but almost by accident one day had a go at hockey. It may have had something to do with the fact that Bill Haddon, the hockey master, and an ex-England player, was also in charge of the young farmers club.

Anyway, I soon gravitated to the left back position and found I quite enjoyed it. I didn't exactly shine at the game but did eventually get into the school 2nd eleven and played a few games against other schools. So hockey and skiing apart, which I took up much later in life and came to enjoy, I have otherwise been a spectator rather than a participant in sports. And when I left school I thought I was too busy to waste time on games. Silly, of course, but it was probably the protestant work ethic that had been crammed into me since childhood. And I do realize I have missed a lot of fun by not being more of a participant.

But my schooldays were not all happy. I was a village boy in an urban environment. I had no experience of how to deal with the frightening aggression of groups of such boys who lived in the same street and went about in gangs. I was a big built boy and could hold my own physically. But I made no more than a handful of lifetime friends at that school because I had little compatibility with most of the other boys.

That is not to say it was not a good school. It was one of the best in Norwich and some of the teachers were excellent. Mr. Beck, for instance, who taught me English for two of my five years at the school, was inspirational. Mr. Cave, made history, come alive and seem totally relevant, especially when he taught us about the agricultural revolution. And there were others to whom I owe a great debt. But by the time I had taken my GCE, aged 15 rather than 16, again because of the accident of my birth date, I could not wait to get away from the place.

Not for me yet more study, yet more exams, followed by the possibility of three years at university. There was no feeling of virtual compulsion to go to university in those days as there is now. That prospect seemed to me aged almost 16 like a waste of time. And although I have regretted not going to university many times since I felt my youth was ebbing away. I had started keeping pigs in my own right when I was ten and by the time I was fifteen they were already beginning to earn quite good money. I thought I was ready to go home to the farm.

Chapter 5

A very young farmer

All through my childhood I had followed my father around the farm, been with him to the blacksmiths, later leading horses there and back on my own, to the village saddler, the machinery dealers, to the market to buy and sell pigs and cattle, and everywhere else I could persuade him to take me.

I drove single horses pulling rolls across a variety of crops. That was my favourite because there was a seat on the back. I drove pairs of horses pulling harrows across fields of barley and wheat – we did that in those days before chemical sprays to try to control weeds – although that meant a lot of walking because there is nowhere to fix a seat on a set of harrows. And I rode on the seat of the binder at harvest time making sure the knife was cutting and the sheaves of wheat, barley and oats were being properly tied with twine.

When I was about ten, I was even given a chance to drive a pair of horses ploughing. If I am honest the team-man in charge walked alongside and kept his hand on the plough and a very close eye on the reins that I was nominally controlling. But I like to think I have a little experience of that ancient art, albeit scant.

The team-man was not always so solicitous. Especially when I volunteered with friends my own age to get the working horses in from pasture first thing on summer mornings. I am afraid we mounted them and either trotted or galloped them up to the stable half a mile away. "You young buggers" he would say when we and our lathered steeds came into the yard "don't you know them hosses ha got a days work to do arter you're done with 'em? You sweat 'em up like that fast thing an' they 'ont be no good fer nothin' arter dinner".

I have always been nostalgic for those days and the horses we shared them with. But when I eventually graduated to driving tractors, which I confess I did at an age that would be illegal today, at least there wasn't the worry of having the team-man watching my every move.

One morning when I was about ten, father and I went to see one of our farming neighbours in the village on some business pretext. His name was Wallace Poll, and he was an old man even then. "Come in and have a cup of tea" he said. Which was probably one of the reasons father had gone to see him. For he was a wise old man who father considered something of a mentor, and he loved to talk farming with him.

As we all sat round his kitchen table talking about the difficult farming years he had lived through several years before, the changes since the outbreak of War and the price of milk (Mr. Poll by this time had a herd of pedigree Dairy Shorthorns) and other matters which were for the most part above me – I heard our host say to my father "You know, Robert, there can sometimes be a difference between a good farmer and a successful farmer".

Precociously I piped up and asked what he meant. For in my young and immature mind a good farmer should be a successful farmer and vice versa.

Patiently the old man explained. "You're too young to remember it" he began "but in the late 1920's and early 30's farming was caught in a deep depression. The value of most farm commodities collapsed. Imports of food flooded in from abroad. There was no market for much of what we produced. And a great many farmers went bankrupt."

"Some of my friends" he continued "carried on farming in traditional ways established over generations. They stuck to the Norfolk Four Course Rotation of Wheat, Beet, Barley, Clover hay, and then back to Wheat again. They retained all their workers, they cut their hedges and dug their ditches every year. They did everything a good farmer should do. But because they were spending more than they were receiving, they went bust. They were good farmers in the conventional sense, but they were not successful."

"I, on the other hand "he went on, "sacked all my men, allowed my hedges to grow unchecked and my ditches to fill up. I put the whole farm down to grass, bought and sold sheep only as and when the price was right, and walked about with a dog and a stick. By the end of the depression, which ended because of the growing threat of war more than anything else, my farm was a mess. I had not been what you would recognize as a good farmer, but I did survive. In that sense I was successful"

At the time of that conversation the recent 2nd World War was dominating the lives of the nation. After the first priority of winning the War, feeding the population came a close second and there was keen demand for everything farmers produced. But I never forgot that old man's wise words. And with variations they remain as true today as they were in the 1940's. The chief lesson is not necessarily that farmers under financial pressure should find the cheapest way to run their farms but that they should not expect to be able to continue in their old ways, no matter what happens. They must be ready to change to survive within the straightened circumstances.

But my weekly trips to Norwich market with my father during the War years had convinced me I should start farming as soon as possible. I persuaded him to sell me my first weaner pig. I also persuaded him to let me have the use of a small sty away from the main farmyard to keep it in. Needless to say, the strict condition of these concessions was that I would feed the pig twice a day and muck it out whenever necessary.

The deal I did with my father involved what we would call today an element of hire purchase. He supplied the pig and the feed and would wait until the animal was sold for bacon for his money. A touch of nepotism crept into the transaction I suspect.

In any event that first pig made me a clear profit, before counting my labour, of around £10. So I immediately began negotiating for my next entrepreneurial venture. The sty was big enough for more than one pig, so I thought it would be a good idea to double up. Those next two pigs made me £8 each, mainly because the notorious pig cycle had kicked in and end prices had slipped a little.

Never mind, I was still well ahead and decided to go for three pigs next time round. They made me £5 each, which was rather disappointing, but by this time I was hooked. And I next persuaded my father to sell me four pigs. But one of them died, destroying any hope of profit from that batch. It was a timely lesson that slowed my headlong expansion, and which demonstrated to me rather painfully that when you keep livestock you sometimes end up with dead stock.

Not long after that I decided to change from pig fattening to pig breeding. I had observed during my visits to Norwich market that the weaners that made the best prices were "blue and whites", the outcome of a cross between a Large White boar and either an Essex or Wessex saddleback sow. I searched around and eventually found a suitable breeding gilt and once again cashing in on my father's good will, by borrowing his boar, was soon producing litters of pigs.

By the time I left the City of Norwich School I had a farrowing shed and about fifteen sows and took pride in the fact that almost every second Saturday I would have a pen of some of the best blue and white weaners in auctioneer Clowes & Nash's pig pens on Norwich market. Pigs were reasonably profitable most of the time in those days and I began to gather together a bit of capital. I thought of myself as a pig farmer as much as a schoolboy. I wanted more to do with pigs and less to do with school.

The other thing that had encouraged me was a trip one December day to the Smithfield Show in London. I don't remember exactly how old I was at the time, but I must have taken time off from school to be there. It was my first time in the Capital and father hadn't been many times either. We travelled on the train from Norwich to Liverpool Street Station. But rather than get lost on the unfamiliar Underground he decided we would take a taxi to Earls Court where the exhibition was being held.

As the taxi driver threaded his way through the crowded streets, the like of which I had never seen before, my father looked out of the window and said "Take a look at all these people walking and riding about here, boy. There's twelve million of 'em in and around this City. And none of 'em know how to grow a 'tater".

He was quite right, of course, and I took that, as he meant me to take it to mean, that farmers would always be wanted to produce the food to feed the masses in this country's cities and towns. What greater vote of confidence in the profession I had already chosen could I have wished for? And for most of the forty or so years that followed he was absolutely right.

But while my father accepted my decision not to stay on at school and try for a place at university, he did draw the line at allowing me to come straight home to the family farm. "You need to have some experience away from here first" he said. "On top of that the time may come when you will employ people to work for you. The best thing you can do is spend some time learning to be employed".

It was one of the best bits of advice I ever had. My father was no fool and he knew that if I came home onto the farm straight from school I might become too sure of myself and that would lead to problems getting on with the workers he employed and with whom I had grown up. He knew some of my rough edges needed knocking off. So he made arrangements for me to work, as an ordinary worker, not a farm pupil, for a 1,500 acre farmer about three miles from home who was well known as an excellent manager of heavy land and also as a strict disciplinarian.

At the same time he persuaded me to agree to attend a day course on agriculture run by the then fairly new Norfolk Agriculture College (now Norfolk's College of the Countryside) and the County Council, which owned the college in the first place. The course took place every Wednesday at the Assembly Rooms in Norwich and ran for three months. Eight of us participated and we were lectured by college staff on each subject in turn. We covered land management, fertility, crop diseases, the management of major species of livestock, landlord/tenant law, agricultural economics and so on. In other words most of the stuff students at agricultural colleges would learn but obviously in less depth. I confess I sometimes wondered at the time why such students needed a couple or more years to learn what we managed in a dozen Wednesdays. Whatever, it was a good course and I enjoyed it. The last session was an exam to see if we had remembered what we had been told and for the first, and I think last, time in my life I got the highest marks.

When the course was over, I reverted to five days a week instead of four on my training farm. My weekly wages during that first year were £3/4s/0, or £3.20p before National Insurance and £3/0s/7, or £3.3p, after this had been deducted. I was making more than that out of my pigs, which I still had to feed and attend to before and after bicycling the three miles to and from the farm where I worked. But I was persuaded it was a good idea and I set about it with enthusiasm.

I was barely sixteen, but a big boy, so tended to be given the heaviest tasks. I well remember a small lad the same age as myself who started the same day I did, on the same pay. But because of his size he was always given light jobs. And, within days I was beginning to see things from the point of view of an employee as well as an employer. It is a discipline I have tried to retain all my working life.

My first job that September of 1953 was to help harvest the potatoes. Each baulk of tubers was spun out by a power-driven spider wheel mounted on the three-point linkage of a little grey Ferguson tractor. A gang of local women picked up the potatoes and put them into open topped wicker baskets weighing about a couple of stones each when full which they left standing on the harvested baulk.

A long-legged Clydesdale horse pulling a tumbril was then put into the row beside where the baskets stood and went at its own pace along the length of the baulk. It was my job to hang onto the back of the tumbril with my left hand, pick up each basket in my right hand as we passed it almost at a run and in one movement swing it up to the small lad riding on the load. By the time they reached him the baskets were empty so all he had to do was catch and throw them down ready to be filled from the next row.

The horses knew that the harder and faster they went the easier the tumbril would pull. And the baskets were often only a few yards apart. There were two horses and two tumbrils, so that while one was being loaded the other was being tipped at the clamp along the edge of the field. No sooner had I finished a strenuous trip up the field than there was another tumbril waiting to be loaded on the way back. My muscles had grown soft during my years at grammar school. But the month I spent on potato lifting soon hardened them again.

On Saturday mornings I was sent cutting marrow stem kale, a member of the cabbage family but with long stems, for the Friesian dairy cows. This involved cutting the two-inch diameter green leaf topped stems as close to the ground as possible and laying them in neat rows ready to be picked up and loaded onto trailers from which they would be spread onto pastures for the weekend feeds.

There were two, for those days, sizeable herds of cows on the farm – one of almost a hundred and another of about eighty head. So they needed a lot of kale to keep them going all weekend and the job usually took me all Saturday morning. It wasn't exactly the reason I had taken the job. I had hoped I might have a rather wider remit and learn about the management of a big farm. But that was what needed to be done, so I did it. However, my objective of seeing as much as possible of the wide range of jobs around the farm was about to take a turn for the worse.

The bigger of the two dairy herds was housed in a traditional shed with cows being tied by the neck in their own stall each time they were milked. The other was a milking parlour, which was like a static milking bail. The cows queued up in a collecting yard to be milked eight at a time. As each cow was milked in the then new-fangled abreast stalls, she would be let out leaving room for the next to come into the same stall – and so on until the whole herd was milked. Three cowmen worked at the cowshed and two in the parlour. There was also a relief milker who was virtually a full-time cowman during the week when he covered for each of the five in turn while they had a day off in lieu of their weekend work.

A few weeks after I started work on the farm there was a bust-up between two of the cowmen who worked in the traditional shed. Apparently one of the younger cowmen, who was, incidentally, married with a family, had been having an affair with the daughter of one of the older cowmen. The young lady was also married to another of the workers on the farm. This was salacious stuff for an innocent sixteen-year-old and was predictably the talk of the farm.

It was clearly a potentially explosive situation and one day it exploded. The cuckolded husband waited around the corner of the hayshed until his young wife's lover came round it on his own, then took his revenge. Suffice to say the randy cowman ended up with a broken jaw requiring hospital treatment and a few weeks off work.

This meant the relief cowman had to become a full-time cowman at the cowshed herd and someone else had to be found to do the relief milking. The foreman turned to me and said I was to be the new relief cowman for both herds. And so it was that I had my first experience of milking cows under two systems of management.

At first, I was entirely happy. I wanted as many varied experiences as possible, and I learned a great deal. The head cowman who could be a bit of a tartar was charming underneath and almost ready to retire. He taught me how to castrate the male calves and dehorn all of them. He showed me how to feed calves to avoid scours and cows to obtain optimum yield. And by example he demonstrated the production of clean milk. But when the young cowman's jaw mended and he came back to work, the father of the young woman he had associated with refused to work with him. The disciplinarian owner of the farm seemed incapable of resolving the matter so the warring parties were kept at opposite ends of the farm and I became semi-permanent as relief milker.

All through the winter I continued to milk cows, first at one herd, then at the other. In order to have the milk churns on the stand by 7.00am, a few minutes before the parlour milk was always collected by the Milk Marketing Board, I was required to be at work in time to get the cows from their meadow into the collecting yard before 5.00am. This meant leaving home by 4.15am at the latest, biking the three miles to the farm, then hustling the cows into the yard ready to be milked. The regime was a little more relaxed at the other farm but it only gave me an extra fifteen minutes in bed on the days I worked there.

I usually arrived home each evening at about quarter to seven, just in time to hear The Archers on the BBC Home Service. It was broadcast

44

a little earlier in the evening in those days. It was a tiring regime for a young boy but I managed to stick it. The trouble was that I was only learning about cows and missing out on all the other things that went on on the farm.

Cowmen had two hours for lunch and while the other chaps went home for their lunch, I would eat my sandwiches in half an hour (usually in the warm tack room where the guvnor's girl groom prepared his horses for hunting) and then walk across the yard to the farm workshop. Jack Halsey who was the farm fitter took to me and in return for my unpaid help he taught me the rudiments of welding and a few other crafts that served me well later in life. But I still felt cheated that my work experience was so restricted.

My father told me not to complain. I had, after all, been told I would have to fit in where I was wanted. But alongside that it was my understanding that every reasonable effort would be made to put me to as many jobs as possible during my year there.

Matters came to a head when, in the following July, while I was still relief milking five days a week, the foreman told me that the following Monday all the cowmen were to take two weeks holiday while most of the cows were drying up (that is coming to the end of their lactation before having their next calf in the autumn) and that I was to fill in as part of the skeleton staff that would look after the cows.

It did not take many seconds to calculate that this would take me through to mid-September. By that time the grain harvest would be over and I would not be involved in any of it. The farm had a combine and a pick-up baler that we did not have at home at the time. Further, that my year on the farm would be finished.

So I told the foreman I refused to do it. To which he replied "I hair wot you say boy. But I dass'nt tell the old man. You'll hatta do it".

And so it was that later that day I found myself outside the office window explaining my reasons for refusing to stay in the cowsheds through harvest. The guvnor was not pleased. He was not used to people standing up to him and I suspect he found it particularly unacceptable from a young boy. Actually, he lost his notoriously quick temper. But although I say it and shouldn't, I was extremely polite but firm and presented him with the options as I saw them. Either I could be given the chance to be involved in the harvest or I could give him notice.

He spluttered a bit then said I should leave. To which I asked whether he would like me to write my notice formally and if he would like me to work out my weeks' notice. Again he spluttered and eventually said I should bring him written notice the following day and work the next week but that it must be among the cows. I accepted his condition and quietly walked away. I had effectively been sacked for the first time in my life. But I felt I had won the moral victory. I never did learn how "the guvnor" really felt. We never spoke of it when we became friends and business colleagues many years later.

Chapter 6

Cows and pigs

Having effectively been dismissed from my first job for insubordination I returned home. If I am honest, it's where I wanted to be, and in spite of my slightly premature arrival my father and the men who worked for him welcomed me back. My absence of a mere ten months had subtly changed my relationship with the men who previously thought of me as the "boss's boy". Now I was also someone who had done a job elsewhere albeit fleetingly. We were close enough for them to have heard on the farmworkers grapevine how I had acquitted myself. And I think there was a sneaking respect for the fact that although I had been asked to leave the job, I had stood up to the notoriously aggressive farmer for whom I had worked and, in effect, left him on my own terms. It was a valuable lesson for me and I have often stressed it to my own children. Time spent working away from the home business is seldom wasted and can be extremely valuable.

Paradoxically, soon after I returned home my father's head cowman decided to leave, which left an automatic vacancy for me to fill. My milking experience during the previous year proved valuable after all and I was able to slot in very easily. The irony of the fact that I had left the last job to get away from cows, albeit to learn other things, was not lost on me but at least these were our own cows and the herd was small enough for me to have time to do other things around the farm as well.

So, here I was aged 17, with less than a years' experience with cows, thrown in at the deep end as head cowman. We ran around 60 Friesians, which was about average for the time and two of us milked them through a twelve-point Alfa Laval milking parlour that my father had bought second hand a few years previously. It was very similar to the one I had worked in on the neighbouring farm. Today when it is commonplace for one man to milk well over a hundred cows on his own through herringbone split level parlours the job probably sounds like it must have been a sinecure.

But standards were different then. The two of us did all the feeding of the cows and their calves as well as keeping the collecting yard clean and, in winter, the lying yards littered. And if, for instance, the visiting threshing contractor was on the farm we would also be called in to cart the corn, in 16 to 18 stone sacks that had to be lifted by hand, from field to barn between milking's. There were extra jobs like that to do quite often so it wasn't the holiday it might seem. And two of us working together was a great deal more pleasant than the loneliness of so many jobs on farms today.

That first autumn I was also in charge of calving's. The heifers were first from mid-September and the cows followed a few weeks later. In those days cows were given names, not numbers, and there were few enough of them that we could easily recognise each one without the need to brand any identification marks on the animal. That year following a policy my father had adopted a few years previously all the heifers were given names beginning with D so that by simply recalling their names we would always know when they had first calved and how old they were.

The very first heifer to calve under my supervision we called Daydream. And she wasn't just the first to have her calf – she was always first in virtually everything she did. Like chickens, cows have a peck-order and even from those youthful days of her first lactation Daydream, who was a fine-looking animal, always led the herd into the collecting yard, was first into the parlour to be milked, first to the trough for her feed and so on. She was also a good milker giving nearly 1,400 gallons in her first lactation, over 1,800 in her second and well over 2,000 in her third. Today those yields would not be remarkable. But in 1955 they were pretty impressive.

Truth be told, Daydream quickly became my favourite cow in the herd and when I discovered her third calf was a bull (by a very good Milk Marketing Board owned sire, by artificial insemination) I persuaded my father to keep it entire and see if we could sell him at Norwich bull sale the following year. The calf had the same bold characteristics as his mother, which is not quite so easy to deal with in a male when, at twelve months he has grown to weigh more than half a tonne. But I was delighted, a year later, when he won second prize at the bull sale and sold for 200 guineas.

Imagine my concern when, one morning, Daydream could hardly stand and was clearly in a lot of pain. The vet was called and he immediately suspected she had swallowed a piece of wire. In those days my father was in the habit of buying hay from other farmers and that year he had bought some baled with wire. The vet suspected that a stray piece had been left in among the fibres of hay and that Daydream being Daydream had gulped hay and wire down together without even realising it. Wire in the stomach was pretty common in those days. It had a cruel effect on cows and in those days before anti-biotics infection could set in and quite often they didn't recover. Nobody was more pleased than me to see the back of wire bales.

To check if his diagnosis was correct the vet had a kind of Geiger-counter that he held under Daydreams' gut. Sure enough it indicated that there was metal in there somewhere and confirmed that an operation to remove it was necessary. It seemed commonplace at the time because such operations were not unusual. But it may be a surprise to some today that the removal of wire from a cow's stomach was done with the animal standing up in her stall and with only a local anaesthetic. This wasn't because the vet was cruel but because only when the patient was standing upright could he get his arm into her stomach to check for foreign objects.

So, Daydream had her operation. The vet shaved her belly just behind her ribs, administered the local anaesthetic, then after a few minutes, cut a long incision in her side. It, and the next incision into the stomach wall, had to be big enough to get his arm inside the cow up to his shoulder. To help in the search for wire the vet had a magnet that he now took in his hand and inserted into the stomach to try to locate the wire. The vet was a Scot called Robbie Asher who was, as usual, full of dirty stories he'd heard on his rounds. As he was fishing for the wire, he regaled us with some of them. I can't claim to remember the jokes that day because I was too concerned about Daydream, but I remember feeling relieved when after a few minutes Robbie pulled out a piece of wire.

"That's the cause of the problem" said Robbie and after ensuring there were no other bits of wire inside the cow, began closing and stitching the wounds. Daydream had stood quietly through all of this, not exactly enjoying the experience I am sure, but tolerating it stoically. Meanwhile Robbie continued closing the wound and reeling off some more of his long list of jokes.

Eventually he said "Right, I think that'll do. I'll just put some sulphanilamide (the cure-all that was used before penicillin) and hope that stops any infection." And with that he began clearing up his instruments. Suddenly he stopped. "Where's my bloody magnet?" he said. But he knew. He had been so pleased to find the wire so quickly and enjoying telling his dirty stories that he had left the magnet in Daydreams' stomach. There was nothing for it but to open her up again to retrieve it. The magnet, if left, could have done almost as much damage as the wire. Although I have heard tell of wrist watches being found in cow's stomachs that must have been there for years that had caused no trouble. One I heard of was supposed to have kept going and was still telling the right time. But that was another vet's tall story, I fear.

Be that as it may, the magnet was found and retrieved and Daydream survived her second operation in as many hours. Three weeks later she was back to her usual place at the head of the herd and almost back to her usual milk yield. What a constitution! What a cow! What a privilege to have known her!

But that first year in charge of the cows was one of the most satisfying of my life. It was hard physical work and long hours but I was able to focus on doing one job as well as possible. I had none of the worries of the rest of the farm and no domestic complications. I was a late developer where girls were concerned, and I was fit and healthy. The heifer's calving's continued with Daphne, Doris, Dawn and so on and then came the older cows. By careful management of the feed the cows were given I was able to claim, by the end of the milk year, that the herd had not only produced more milk than ever before but that they had done it more economically. My father was pleased and had no hesitation in asking me to carry on in charge of the cows. I did it for three years before we agreed that I should leave the milking to someone else and move on to another enterprise on the farm. In some ways I didn't want to relinquish the cows because in spite of the early mornings and weekend work, I had been able to focus on them, improve their performance and derive a great deal of job satisfaction from managing them.

One reason for changing my role on the farm was because we (father regarded me as part of the management by this time) had decided to expand the pig herd. We had run about forty breeding sows for several years but we could see from the limited returns we were getting from them that we needed to double the numbers. Aged twenty, therefore, and coincidental with another staff change, this time in the pig department, I was transferred from managing cows to pigs and to oversee the construction of more breeding and fattening buildings.

My informal training in the basics of building taught me by my maternal grandfather came in handy as, between feeding the pigs twice a day, supervising farrowing's, injecting iron into piglets to prevent anaemia and so on, I helped a couple of freelance builders from the village put up the extra accommodation we needed. I had an insatiable appetite for physical work in those days and only wish I still had it today. I had worked off all the puppy fat that had made cross-country running such a burden in my school days and I felt myself to be lean, fit, and full of energy.

My father knew a bit about pigs. He had kept them since he was a boy, as I had, and he insisted that they be fed on wet feed. That is to say meal mixed with water into a kind of porridge. Some pig farmers had already turned to feeding dry meal to reduce the hard labour of pig feeding but father was convinced the dust this generated led to lung problems. He was right, of course. Others had begun to feed pellets but these were more expensive and there could still be dust problems. So, apart from the new-born pigs that were fed tiny pellet pencils to supplement their mother's milk, our pigs had wet feed.

Today wet feeding is still popular for the same reasons my father favoured it. But it has been mechanised by fitting large paddles into big tanks and mixing water and meal together to be pumped through plastic pipelines to each pigpen in turn. The entire operation is computer controlled with exactly the right amount of water and meal being delivered to each trough according to the number and size of pigs in the pen. It's all electronically controlled in the mixing shed and so automated has it become that pigs can be fed at any time of day or night without the need for anyone to be there.

It wasn't like that in 1956. We used to mix the meal from straight ingredients in a one tonne electrically driven mixer. That in itself was a luxury. Only a few years before we had been mixing it on the barn floor with shovels. The meal was bagged off into sacks that contained about 12 stones and when we were ready to feed, we tipped a predetermined number of them into a large bath of water on wheels. The "porridge" was then thoroughly shovel mixed to a consistency that would allow a bucket to be dipped into it to ladle it out into the pig's troughs. But the full bath was far too heavy to push round the farmyard. So we had a pony that we harnessed onto the front of the bath and it pulled the feed to where we wanted it.

When the pony was in a good mood the system worked well. But if, for some reason, he was a bit tetchy, he would snatch forward on his traces as he pulled the bath out of the mixing shed and the pigman walking behind and trying to steady the bath with one hand and drive the pony with the other would have his boots filled with pig feed as it spilled over the back. Not a pleasant experience, especially when it happens on the first load and you know there are another half dozen loads to do to feed the herd.

This was the job I inherited. It was hard grinding work with shovelling and lifting integral to almost everything about it. I had liked pigs all my life, so being among them and looking after them was not too much of a burden. But after a few months I began to experience a return of the back trouble that I had first stirred up when carrying 18 stone sacks of wheat up granary steps and tipping them into a bulk heap beside the hammer mill between milking's.

One day I was walking across the yard carrying a big bucket of wet feed in each hand trying to ignore the pain in my lower back when I literally seized up. I just stood there and could not move my legs. I had the presence of mind to drop the buckets which promptly fell over spilling their contents all over the yard. But I still could not move until another man came into the yard on a tractor and after having a good laugh at my plight, realised I was in trouble and helped me to stagger into the barn. Eventually the worst of the spasm left me and I was able to totter into the farmhouse.

I was young and after a few days rest I was back to work as hard as ever. I did not go to the doctor because I was too stubborn. I had delighted in my strength and ability to lift and carry more than most chaps my age since I was a boy and I was not about to let a pulled muscle in my back stop me from doing what I wanted to do. In reality, of course, I had slipped a disc, aged only 19 and that episode was the first of several painful bouts of spasms and worse that have recurred throughout my life – usually when I have been working too hard or been careless with lifting.

I didn't realise it at the time but my weakened back was to play a key role in bringing about significant changes in my life several years later.

Chapter 7

Feeling my feet

My teenage slipped disc forced me to slow down a bit; to use my head more and my hands (and back) a little less. The orthopaedic specialist at the hospital fitted me with a plastic corset moulded round my body and I was told to wear it at work and avoid lifting heavy weights. It was OK in the winter but hell in the summer and soon became saturated in my sweat. Before long it became rather smelly and I was feeling better anyway so discarded it especially when I went out to Norwich on Saturday nights.

My early teens had been fairly quiet with most of my social life associated with the Methodist Church at Hethersett. My father ran a male voice choir, which I joined soon after my voice broke, and we travelled all over Norfolk giving concerts, usually to help raise money for other churches. The hairs on the back of my neck still stand up when I hear a Welsh male voice choir on the radio making the kinds of magnificent sounds which we tried but often failed to emulate. The Glasgow Orpheus Choir was another that my father used as a target for our group and although we failed to come up to their levels of excellence, we can't have been too bad or we wouldn't have been invited to perform all the concerts we did over so many years. In truth, my father's excellent bass voice, his sister Bessie's skilled accompaniment and deep contralto, and their sister Annie's rich soprano – the three sang trios between the male voice items - made up for some of the inadequacies of the rest of us.

But by the time I was 18 my hormones had kicked in and made me want to seek out new experiences. OK, I was a late developer. In any event I started dancing classes in Norwich on Saturday evenings. It was all very innocent stuff by today's standards but it did allow me to embrace several pretty girls each lesson without getting my face slapped. And when the lessons were over a group of us used to spend the rest of the evening in a coffee bar called the Copper Kettle. This was exciting stuff for a naïve country boy in the 1950's and I loved it.

At about the same time I joined Wymondham Young Farmers Club, a few miles along the A11 in the opposite direction from Norwich, where I was able to meet more girls, this time with farming connections, and other farmers sons from around the area, most of whom (male and female) are friends to this day. I think it must have been at about the third meeting I'd attended when the secretary, Rosemary Colchester, came up to me as it was about to start and asked me to propose the vote of thanks to that evening's speaker.

I had never done anything like it before and I was terrified. But before I could decline Rosemary had gone off to start the meeting with the chairman and I knew I had to do it or look an even bigger fool than I already felt. What made it even more nerve-wracking was that the speaker that evening was a man called Hubert Mitchell who was the County Drama organiser for Norfolk County Council who was there to give us a talk on Effective Public Speaking.

During his presentation he stressed again and again that speakers who wished to communicate with their audience must not be pompous or affected. "Keep your message simple and ensure, without talking down to them, that everyone understands what it is you want to say. Never use long words when short ones will do just as well" he told us "and whatever you do avoid fancy phrases."

I needed a hook from his speech on which to base what I had to say and I chose that thought. When I stood up, trembling, to propose my vote of thanks I began "Far be it from me to attempt to compete with Mr Mitchell's wealth of vocabulary and scintillating wit with my humble phraseology..."

Obviously I was poking gentle fun at the speaker but also myself by pretending not to have understood what he had said. But I had no idea if it would be thought amusing or be appreciated. To my amazement and delight everybody, including the speaker, began to laugh and I loved this first experience of amusing people. It is something I have tried to develop since. For in my view humour is the oil that makes the mechanics of human relations function. Without it life is dry, boring, less enjoyable and less efficient.

I look back on my years in the Young Farmers Club with gratitude and affection. In some ways it became for me the university I never attended. In those days there were only a few agricultural colleges and university departments specialising in the subject. Only the sons (and a very few of the daughters) of well to do and wealthy farmers went to places like Cirencester for further farming education. My father was not of that group and as already explained, I thought I had had my fill of education and only wanted to go farming. But I shall always be grateful to the distinguished farmers and others who came to our Club on Monday evenings to share their knowledge and experiences – some serious, some amusing, but almost always educational.

It is important to realise that Young Farmers Clubs are self-governing. There is a system of mentoring with a County Organiser (these days often called a Co-ordinator) at the centre and volunteer leaders in every club. But they are there mainly to advise and guide. They do not do everything for the members who elect officers each year from among their number and self-reliance is the name of the game. Our Club Leader, local farmer and ex member, the late John Dring, was a few years older than most of the rest of us and was a great motivator. Our County Organiser was Gordon Mosley, a farmer's son from Derbyshire, who also became a great friend and colleague – more of him later. I'm not sure we ordinary club members realised just how privileged we were at the time but we certainly know it now.

By the time I was 19 I had been elected chairman of the Wymondham club. This meant organising and controlling the weekly meeting – often numbering 60 or more – as well as welcoming and introducing speakers. It also involved chairing club committee meetings and representing the club on County committees. Young Farmers was, and I believe still is, a wonderful training ground. Looking back on such experiences I often wonder at how I, and others of my tender years, were able to manage meetings and reach important decisions affecting many other young people. Once again I had been pushed in at the deep end and had to learn to swim. But I did it and still remember and use the lessons I learned in those early days.

The success of my maiden public speech persuaded my fellow Young Farmers that I should be pushed into doing more and before long I was representing the Wymondham club in stock judging competitions against other clubs. I remember winning the Norfolk Dairy Cow judging on one occasion and bringing home a handsome silver cow on a plinth. It sat proudly on our mantelpiece for a year. Another time I was joint winner of the county pig judging competition with my friend Rex Webster and that summer we travelled around East Anglia judging for Norfolk against Young Farmers in other counties. It was one of the most enjoyable times of my life.

During the same period I was entered into a public speaking

competition to represent my club. It was held in an ex-army wartime Nissan hut at what later became Wymondham College – now a highly successful residential school. The surroundings were drab but we Young Farmers were oblivious to that. We were having fun and learning at the same time.

One of the things we had to do in the competition was to draw a subject out of a hat and speak on it immediately for two minutes. I don't remember my subject but my friend and rival, Benny Gaze from the Diss club, drew the subject "A Farmers Garden". Like a shot Benny stood up and began to speak. "I would like to speak to you about a farmer's garden" he began. "But first I want us to consider – what is a typical farmer's garden? I suggest it is three of sand and one of cement…."

Benny was quick witted and always good value in such situations as were many of my other contemporaries of those days and listening to them was always a joy. But although I have no recollection on what I spoke about my biggest thrill that day was winning the county competition and the small shield I was awarded stands on our mantelpiece to this day.

Perhaps because I was unable to keep my mouth shut I was elected by my club to serve on the County Executive Committee – the body that governed Young Farmers affairs in Norfolk. I relished being at the centre of things and helping to organise events and it wasn't long before I was made Vice Chairman of the committee and then, a year later, Chairman of the County. It was a proud moment and I soon found myself representing Young Farmers in a wide range of situations and mixing with some of the top people in Norfolk agriculture.

One of my duties was to support our County Organiser, Gordon Mosley, as he sought to start YF clubs in Norfolk towns that didn't have one. One such was Thetford, just down the road from Wymondham, where he was convinced there was a good nucleus of potential members and he asked if I and a few other Wymondham members would join him at the inaugural meeting.

About fifteen or twenty interested young people turned up and after we'd had a good discussion it was agreed to start a club based around the town. The Wymondham contingent, including myself, agreed to keep an eye on it for a few months attending meetings when we were able. We then turned to the task of electing the first officers of the new club. A likely looking chap who'd had a bit to say volunteered to be chairman and then a good-looking girl at the back, who nobody seemed to know, offered to act as secretary. And the Thetford club was born.

Being a conscientious sort of chap I went to several meetings to ensure they were getting on OK. Indeed after a few weeks I was the only outsider still attending. And I have to confess, although I was keen to see the club progress, my main interest became the new secretary. Her name was Lorna Young. She had only recently moved to the Thetford area from Cumberland with her mother and younger sister where her father had farmed. Sadly, he had recently died and Mrs Young had brought her daughters back to her home to live with her bachelor brother who farmed nearby.

Lorna, still devastated by her father's death, needed to establish a new life in a new area and chose Young Farmers as the place to start. Suffice to say I was pleased to help and we got married in Bury St Edmunds Cathedral the following January.

Chapter 8

I acquire a farm, and a wife

One of the meetings I chaired at Wymondham Young Farmers Club during my year in office was addressed by Vice Admiral Sir Edward Evans-Lombe, a local landowner and the landlord of the farm my father had rented many years before. But his subject when he spoke to the club was not land or farming but the defence of Western Europe against the USSR. This was the time of the Cold War with the Soviet Union and following a distinguished career in the Navy he had been asked by the government to take charge of NATO forces in Northern Europe and he had been based for several years in Norway.

By the time he came to speak to us he had retired from that post too, but I vividly remember that he gave us a fascinating insight into European politics, nuclear defence strategies and so on. He was a big man – about 6ft 4inches – with a big and authoritative voice and it was a real privilege to listen to him. Moreover, although my father had obviously met him on several occasions it was the first time I had spoken to him.

Some months later I heard on the local grapevine that an elderly farmer in the next village, called George Huggins, was giving up the tenancy of Whiterails Farm, Great Melton and that the estate was looking for a new tenant. The farm ran to some 260 acres of mainly medium quality Grade III land and not to put too fine a point on it, it had not been well farmed for years. The hedges were without exception about twelve feet high and just as wide. The ditches were nearly level full. And every field grew a mat of twitch, or spear grass as we call it in Norfolk. It was hardly a peach of an opportunity, especially in those days before mechanised hedging and ditching and when Roundup (the chemical we now use to kill twitch) had not been invented. But it was only a mile or so from our existing land and it had a good house. So I applied for the tenancy.

Whether my contact with the landowner at the Young Farmers Club had anything to do with it I can't say but a few weeks later my father and I were invited to meet the estates agent and he offered to rent us the farm at £4/acre. He made the point that, as I was only twenty, the landowner would feel happier if it were a joint tenancy between my father and myself for the time being and that, all other things being equal, when my father retired or died I would become the sole tenant. We accepted, then went away to raise the money for working capital.

My pig farming activities had enabled me to raise a small nest egg of about £1,500 which I put into the pot and we persuaded Kenneth Riches, the headmaster-like manager at our branch of Barclays Bank in Norwich to provide an overdraft of £7,000 which we believed, with other changes we had planned, would be enough to carry us through to the first harvest. Together with the 137 acres of estate land father was already farming and other bits and pieces that he owned and rented we would now be farming nearly 440 acres which, in 1958 was a fair-sized farm.

Those changes included selling the dairy cows and simplifying the arable rotation enabling us to reduce our labour bill. My confidence in proposing these measures to my father was boosted by contacts I had made through Young Farmers with local ADAS officers. They were getting to grips with a new concept that had been recently launched by the service called Gross Margins. Every farmer worth his salt uses a version of the system these days to assess the relative profitability of different enterprises. It involved separating what were deemed variable costs for things like seed, fertilisers, chemicals from so called fixed costs such as labour, depreciation, rent and so on. It's all very familiar now but in 1958 it was new and I must have been one of the first ADAS "clients" to volunteer to use it, first on a theoretical basis in anticipation of taking Whiterails Farm then later using the actual figures for what we spent and produced.

The exercise showed we had been trying too hard. On our relatively small acreage we had been running a herd of dairy cows, a herd of breeding pigs with all the progeny being finished for bacon and a flock of breeding hens producing hatching eggs for a local hatchery. On the arable land we grew wheat, barley, oats, sugar beet, and potatoes. And to do all the work there was a workforce of about eight men on top of the contributions father and I made.

It all sounds transparently ridiculous now and inevitably some of those enterprises made money while others were losing. But father had lived and farmed through the 1930's depression before the days of marketing boards and guaranteed prices. In those days of volatile and often very low prices for farm commodities the received wisdom accepted by most farmers was that it was risky to put all your eggs in one basket. But father had rather overdone the risk spreading and the Gross Margin calculations showed that the time had come to simplify and cut costs.

We had an auction on the farm to sell the cows. My time in charge of the herd had made me fond of them and it was a bit emotional. But they weren't as profitable as they should have been and in any case we needed the money to fund the new farm. The breeding poultry went as well although we did stay in the egg business producing on deep litter to sell to the Egg Marketing Board. We decided to keep the pigs with a view to expanding the size of the herd.

We cut out oats and potatoes from the arable rotation leaving just wheat, barley and sugar beet. And we were able to reduce the labour force, despite the fact that we were taking on more land. Like losing the cows, that was not easy. Father prided himself on his relationship with the men. Indeed he had worked alongside them for years. I feared I would be viewed as the ruthless young pup who'd come home to upset a happy crew. But the figures showed it had to be done and to my surprise the men who left as well as those who stayed respected me for doing it. Those men knew, without the benefit of Gross Margins, that the management needed a shake-up and they accepted what I had to do. Fortunately, all of those we asked to leave were able to get other jobs in the district in a matter of weeks.

And so, in the autumn of 1958, we set about the new farm. We cultivated the stubbles to try to control the twitch, we hired a contractor to cut the hedges back to a reasonable size with a circular saw. It was a vicious tool and would probably be illegal today. But it let the light into our fields and we've managed our hedges for wildlife and efficient farming ever since. And we employed three itinerant Irishmen, complete with shovels, to spend the winter digging ditches. By the following spring the farm was starting to look better than when we'd arrived.

Through all of this activity I had continued courting Lorna. She worked as a matron at the East Anglian School for Girls at Bury St Edmunds in Suffolk, which was twinned with the famous Culford School for Boys just outside the town. It was forty miles each way to visit her and given how busy I was on the farm and with Young Farmers duties time spent with her was limited. But there was a big house on Whiterails

Farm and one of the clauses in the tenancy agreement stated that I must live in it. I didn't much want to be there alone and I couldn't afford a housekeeper so it seemed like a good idea to get married. Lorna agreed and so began a partnership that, lasted nearly 60 years until she sadly died in August 2018.

January 16th, 1959 was a cold, snowy day in Bury St Edmunds. I had persuaded my friend Alan Alston to be my Best Man. That friendship lasted even longer than my marriage. We met in Young Farmers before I knew Lorna and we had lunch together, with our wives, virtually every Saturday. But that day we sat side by side in Bury St Edmunds Cathedral, shivering slightly, either with the cold or nerves or both, waiting for the bridal party to arrive. The appointed time for the service was long gone and we both kept looking at our watches wondering which of a number of possibilities had happened. Either Lorna had changed her mind, or the Rolls Royce booked for her journey had gone off the road having skidded on the ice, or she was overdoing the bride's privilege of being a few minutes late.

Fortunately, the delay was caused by the last of those and Lorna was aided and abetted in her lateness by her cousin, Willy Young, who was to give her away. Willy worked for the Ministry of Agriculture as a livestock licencing officer in Gloucestershire. In other words he visited farms assessing the quality of pedigree bulls, rams, and boars that farmers wanted to keep for breeding and either granting a licence, or not, if he judged the animal unsuitable. Those males that passed muster were marked with an official tattoo in their ear. It was part of the Ministry's campaign to improve the standard of the nation's livestock. Today, such judgements are left to farmers themselves. But it was a valuable exercise at the time.

Willy was Scottish (like Lorna) and something of a comedian. He joked that I had undergone the same sort of inspection he made on bulls, rams and boar's and drew attention to the tattoo he said he had put in my ear. He was my kind of man and we got on famously from the first time we met. Sadly, both he and his wife Phyllis were killed in a car accident well into their retirement. But that day he had told the driver of the Rolls in which he and Lorna were travelling to go round the block a couple of times "to make the bugger wait a bit – he'll appreciate you more".

I'd arranged a honeymoon in London. We stayed at the Russell Hotel in Russell Square. It was the only one I knew at the time having stayed there a few times when on Young Farmers business. What I wasn't aware of was that our wedding had coincided with the national NFU AGM and the hotel was full of farmers attending the meeting. Furthermore, Lorna's late father had been active in the NFU having been County Chairman of Cumberland before he fell ill and some of the delegates from the county recognised her. One in particular, Joe Ewing, came over to congratulate us on our marriage and insisted that he would treat us to dinner at his club.

That night he took us to this select little club at the back of the Dorchester Hotel. The food was excellent, the piano playing just right to create an attractive atmosphere and what it all cost I have no idea. But it won't have been cheap. Indeed during the evening Joe was presented with a bill for a bunch of other dinners he'd hosted in the place and I was shocked when I saw across the table the size of the cheque he wrote to pay it. I wondered how he could afford such extravagance on a farmer's income and my suspicions were confirmed a few years later when we heard he'd gone out of business. But it was a memorable evening and I shall never forget Joe striding across Park Lane, arms akimbo, whistling as to a sheepdog on a distant hill for a taxi to take us back to our hotel.

The rest of the honeymoon was a bit of a blur. I remember that we went to a couple of West End shows – West Side Story and The Boyfriend. We visited Madame Tussaud's and the Planetarium, had a few modest meals at places like Aberdeen Angus Steak Houses and after four days we ran out of money so we came back to Norfolk. The builders who were getting the farmhouse ready for us were a bit surprised because they hadn't finished their work. But the kitchen and the main bedroom were ready so we made ourselves as comfortable as we could and with the sound of concrete mixers and carpenters saws in the background, set up home together.

Chapter 9

Whiterails – the first year

That first year at Whiterails was unmitigated hard work. Everything was new, including managing men, and had to be thought about and decided upon for the first time. And although I had enormous support from my father I was ultimately in charge – he saw to that. Unlike some farming fathers I've come across over the years he wanted to give me responsibility for decision making. He didn't cling to power or the cheque book. He allowed me to make my own mistakes and resisted the temptation to say – I told you so.

But he had suggested we should employ the foreman who'd been in charge of the farm in the absence of the retiring tenant. I commented that he hadn't made much of a job of it or the place would have looked tidier. But father pointed out that the man had been on the farm for a few years and knew the land, where the wet holes were and so on and that we should glean this knowledge from him. He was also an experienced combine harvester driver. We realised we would have to buy one to deal with our expanded acres of cereals and since up to that point we had used a self-binder to cut and tie up sheaves that were later stacked to be threshed through a contractor's drum during the winter and had no experience of combines it seemed sensible to keep him on.

My relationship with this man was difficult from the start. In his eyes, as the man who knew the farm and set the men to their various jobs each morning, he was the boss and I was just the boy. I remembered my time spent as a worker on the neighbour's farm after I left school and tried to put myself in his position to understand how he felt about his change of status. Someone younger – I was still only 21 - and less experienced than he was had been made his boss. And as a rather overconfident, not to say big headed chap he was not comfortable with his situation.

There were a few sharp exchanges between us but we managed to work together through that first year without too many rows. And I was grateful to him for helping to select the second hand combine we bought to gather the 1959 harvest. It was a Claas SF bagger machine with a 10ft cutter bar that had already done a few harvests. Compared with today's combine's, which are huge with cutter bars of 30ft or more and can cut and harvest 50t/hour it was tiny. But to us in those relatively early days of combine development, it was magnificent.

It was also the biggest combine the foreman had driven and he claimed it as his baby from the day it arrived. He insisted that he was the only person on the farm that could drive it and that while he was having his midday meal and afternoon tea the combine would stop. This would clearly mean wasting many hours of sunny weather through the course of a harvest which I was not prepared to allow. So I made him teach me how to drive the machine so as to be able to keep it going during his breaks. It was yet another cause of tension between us.

In truth it wasn't a very pleasant job. The driving platform of that model sat immediately over the cutting table above the inlet to elevator that took the crop up into the threshing drum. As anyone who has ever watched a combine work will know this, apart from the rear end, is the place where muck and dust rises the entire time the machine is working. It was necessary for the driver to dress in clothes that protected him as much as possible from this filth. I wore the oldest trousers I could find, a pyjama jacket buttoned up to the neck, a silk scarf over my mouth and nose, stone breakers glasses to protect my eyes, and a baseball cap on my head. After a few hours on the driver's seat you were covered in dust and chaff and while the silk scarf stopped some of it being breathed into your lungs, it didn't stop it all and by the end of the day you were usually wheezing and coughing.

Behind the driver's platform was a bagging mechanism to fill the then universally used comb sacks weighing 16 to 18 stone when full. Another man had to stand on the moving machine supervising the filling of these, tying the tops securely with string, then lugging them manually to the edge of the platform on which he worked before pushing them down a chute onto the ground. Other men then had to follow the combine picking up the full sacks of grain. We managed to buy an old Albion lorry fitted with a hydraulic sack hoist which lifted the sacks, one at a time, so that a man riding on the lorry could take them on his back and stack them on the lorry which then delivered them to the barn. When I wasn't driving the combine I was usually the man on the lorry. My back, injured a year or two previously, ached a bit but the job had to be done. It was hard, dirty work in the harvest field in those days.

But we thought it was wonderful and so much better than the old self-binder and stacking sheaves we'd been used to. Today, the whole business is mechanised and grain is handled in bulk. The combine driver sits in air-conditioned luxury alongside a computer that tells him everything he needs to know about what he's doing. At a glance he can tell the moisture of the grain, how many tonnes per hour he's harvesting, how many hectares and tonnes he's done that day, and so on. Once he's set the machine into work he presses a button and automatic steering takes over. And if he's thirsty he can reach into the on-board refrigerator for his drink.

Grain is collected in a tank on top of the machine – perhaps 10 or more tonnes of it. And when the tank is full it's moved by an auger in a spout out to a trailer running alongside. It in turn is taken to the barn and tipped into a pit from where it is elevated and conveyed to where it's to be stored. And there's not a sack in sight. How times have changed!

That first harvest of 1959 was one of the easiest, weather wise, I've ever known. The sun shone; the yields were quite good; the grain was dry; and we were able to work virtually every day until it was finished. By August 25th it was done. I haven't known many like it in all the years I've been farming.

It was a satisfying first year during which we'd had a few problems but they'd been overcome. One of those problems was when the bank manager telephoned to ask why we'd exceeded our overdraft limit. Apparently a cheque we'd written in the July, just before harvest, had taken us about £50 over the agreed level." Come in and see me tomorrow morning and tell me what you're going to do about it", he said. This was the age of the credit squeeze when bankers could and sometimes did demand overdrafts be reduced overnight and clients who were undisciplined enough to fail to stay within their limits were carpeted.

Next morning was a bit like going in front of a Headmaster. "I advanced you money because I thought I could trust you", said Kenneth Riches. "As a tenant farmer you understand very well that I didn't do it on the basis of the security you could offer. And you've let me down." And he went on "I still think you're capable of controlling your expenditure as we agreed but before I allow you to continue the arrangement I need to know precisely what you intend to do to bring the account back under the overdraft limit. And I want you to satisfy me that the money coming in will exceed that going out". And I was then required to spell out in detail how I expected the farm's cash flow to look over the next few months. It was tough and it was embarrassing. But it taught me a lesson I have remembered. And I often wonder as I look at the financial crises that affect individuals, companies, and nations in these "more enlightened" times might have been avoided if more people had been disciplined by Kenneth Riches.

Be that as it may, back then at the end of August 1959 we had more grain in the barn than I'd anticipated and I was confident we could comply with the Bank's wishes. So I suggested to Lorna that we take a few days off before the autumn drilling needed to be done to visit her old stamping grounds and some of her relatives and friends who had not made it to the wedding the previous January. She jumped at the chance and off we went leaving the farm men to cultivate stubbles and try to kill some more of that twitch that hadn't gone away.

We headed first for Carlisle, or rather a small village beside it called High Heskett, so she could visit the grave where her late father, James Young (and many members of his family) was buried. A number of cousins lived around Carlisle so they had to be visited as well, then on to Gretna where there were one or two more and beyond to Dumfries and Ayr where she had gone to school. I had the dubious pleasure of being introduced to her Head Mistress who remembered Lorna for two main reasons. She had broken a glass door and cut her arm badly when she and a bunch of girls had been misbehaving and was very nearly expelled. And she had been the star pianist of her year. In any event Miss Donnachie greeted us warmly over a cup of coffee and we went on our way.

A fair proportion of Lorna's relatives were farmers or associated with the industry and I was in my element walking round their farms, looking at their beautiful cattle, (mostly Ayrshires) and talking farming. My main problem, however, was sorting out relationships, distinguishing between first and second cousins and remembering how they all fitted together. I realised I didn't possess the kind of memory most of those Ayrshire breeders had to be able to walk onto a meadow full of cows and tell, without reference to record books, which calf came from which mother and how the lineage of the whole herd could be traced back to some bull back in history. I developed the same kind of confusion about Lorna's relations on that trip and although I've sussed most of them out over the years I'm not entirely confident I have them all right even now.

Back in Norfolk we got ready to launch into our second year at Whiterails. My confidence was growing and I had definite ideas on how certain jobs should be organised and done. But the foreman I'd inherited, who had been blocking me on several matters for a year, did not agree with some of them. He went so far as to tell me I was talking rubbish and refused to do what I had asked. I felt I had no alternative but to tell him our relationship wasn't working and that it was time we parted company. I gave him a month's notice (you could do that in those days). He was clearly shocked and unwilling to accept it. He got on his motor bike and I later learned headed off to my father's house. There he apparently told father what had happened and that the notice must be reversed to avoid the farm going to rack and ruin. To which father apparently replied that I had authority to hire and fire and if I felt he should go then he must go. And after an uncomfortable month while the now ex foreman cleared up his belongings (but didn't work) he did.

Father told me later that he had anticipated that what happened would happen but had not interfered so as to allow me time to build up enough confidence to do what was necessary. He was not a dominant father but he was a wise old bird and I was lucky to have him.

Meanwhile the farm began to build a momentum. We had, during the previous year, increased the size of the pig breeding herd and converted most of the traditional buildings – put up in Victorian times – for pig fattening. They were no good for contemporary arable farming because they weren't high enough to tip a trailer or big enough to manoeuvre machines inside. But with a bit of modest modification and the addition of water drinking bowls they were ideal for finishing bunches of pigs – 40 to 60 according to their variable size – on straw. They served us in that way for many years.

The single suckler Blue Grey Cows I'd bought from St Boswell's market in Scotland in the autumn of 1958 had all produced excellent calves and they were being fattened satisfactorily in a yard at Whiterails. Their mothers were happily grazing water meadows, which were the reason they'd been bought, although I was a little concerned at whether or not they were all in calf. We'd acquired a five-year-old Aberdeen Angus bull from a Norfolk dealer to serve them and although he had an excellent conformation I was not convinced he was doing his job as enthusiastically as he should. As it turned out when we asked the vet to do a pregnancy test on the herd only about half were in calf.

Emergency measures were called for and we enquired about the availability of alternative beef bulls in the district. We heard from friends about a four-year-old White Shorthorn bull at Bintry near Fakenham in Norfolk and arranged to go and see it. It was owned by Mr Robert Seaman, an elderly member of a famous Norfolk farming and milling family, who took father and me out onto his water meadows to inspect the bull. He was a beautiful animal. Pure white with meat in all the places butchers like it to be. It was a few years before Charolais cattle were imported from France but when they were they were very much the same stamp as the bull we were inspecting.

Conscious of the problems we'd had with the Aberdeen Angus I complemented Mr Seaman on his bull but asked "Is he fertile and good at his job?" Mr Seaman looked me in the eye, put his hand on my arm and said, "My boy, that animal will bull a cow at twenty mile an hour". We bought him and I have to admit Mr Seaman was right.

I'm pleased to say that I, apparently, had more in common with the White Shorthorn than the Aberdeen Angus because Lorna was pregnant and our first son, Andrew, was born in March 1960.

Chapter 10

Introduction to TV and journalism

Having been Vice Chairman of Norfolk Young Farmers when I moved to Whiterails I had, by this time, been elected Chairman. This meant not only chairing county meetings, attending NFU and other events representing the County Federations and various other duties, but also visiting all the county's' clubs to tell them what was going on at county headquarters and drumming up support for the activities that were centrally arranged. It took me away from the farm a great deal although fortunately most meetings were in the evenings. I was conscious that I was leaving Lorna to fend for herself and the new baby more than I should but as a Young Farmer herself she gave me her blessing. But I was spending a lot on petrol for the car and although the cost was coming out of the farm I felt guilty, not least because I was enjoying it so much. But luckily father backed what I was doing as well, so I carried on.

And so we arrived at my second harvest. The weather was nothing like as kind as it had been for the first with interruptions for rain causing delays to combining. That was why I was cement rendering that grain pit on the August day when Dick Joice called.

He and I became close friends over the next few years. Like me he'd begun life as a working farmer. He was also something of an inventor and liked nothing better than to muck about in his farm workshop making kit to use on his farm. He showed me all kinds of gadgets he'd made, including a machine to single sugar beet. In those days we planted natural sugar beet seeds that had multiple germs grouped together within one crust. This meant the plants were too close together when they emerged and had to be hand singled by men with hoes – a laborious, costly and time-consuming job. Today the seed trade supplies single germ seeds which are coated to a regular size and shape with a clay substance which melts when it is moistened by the soil. This enables specially designed machines to plant the right number of seeds at the correct spacing for an optimum crop. But back in the early 1960's Dick invented a machine that when towed along the rows of sugar beet by a tractor would thin the densely populated rows of plants to almost the desired density. Another of his hobbies was photography including movie photography and he even had a shop in Fakenham that sold cameras.

He was a tenant on the Raynham estate and had become friendly with his landlord, Lord Townshend, a descendant of the famous Turnip Townshend who pioneered the feeding of turnips to sheep in the late 18th century foreshadowing the development of the Norfolk Four Course Crop Rotation. But more than 150 years later his successor was chairman of a consortium that had won the ITV franchise to run Anglia Television. The consortium consisted of film people from Elstree Studios, one or two ex BBC News people, Aubrey, later Lord, Buxton who went on to make Survival films of wildlife around the world, and Lord Townshend.

As I understand it the rest of the consortium said to Lord Townshend, "Leave the news and drama to us. You sort out a programme for farmers" Doubtless it was more complicated than that but it's what happened. Lord Townshend, knowing of Dick Joice's interest in film, asked him to go with him to London to look at some programmes done by one or two other ITV companies that were already up and running. They watched some presented by the then famous commentator Franklin Engelmann entitled The Other Man's Farm, for instance, and on the way home on the train Lord Townshend asked Dick, as a working farmer, what he thought of them.

Dick gave his opinion on what was right and wrong with what they'd seen and how it could be done better, especially for an East Anglian audience, and by the time the train arrived back in Norwich, Lord Townshend said, "Well Dick, you're the obvious man to present it".

And so Farming Diary was born. It was first transmitted on a Sunday lunchtime in the autumn of 1959 with Dick Joice as chairman and interviewer. What Lord Townshend had not appreciated was that Dick was slightly dyslexic and found it difficult to read a script. But that didn't matter much because Dick had a remarkable memory and was soon able to talk to the camera as if to an old friend. And when things went wrong, as they often did in those early days of black and while television, he could extemporise and still look professional. In short, he was a natural and quickly became Anglia's most popular presenter.

As already explained, we had no mains electricity at Whiterails for the first few years so no television either. We couldn't have afforded one anyway. So my knowledge of Dick and Farming Diary was limited to the times Lorna and I were invited to Sunday lunch with my parents.

Indeed I was appearing regularly on TV for a couple of years before we were connected to mains electricity and were able to buy our first TV.

But I couldn't help wondering why I of all the people they might have picked had been chosen to appear on TV so I asked Dick how it had happened. Anglia was very much a junior in the broadcasting business, operating as they did in a relatively sparsely populated area of the country, and were keen to start new programmes as quickly as advertising revenue allowed. The BBC, at the time, were enjoying great success with the Tonight programme, hosted by Cliff Michelmore, and the powers at Anglia fancied emulating it with an east Anglian version with Dick Joice as the front man.

Even at this early stage in Anglia's development Dick, the natural broadcaster, was becoming quite powerful. Asked to take on the much greater burden of work that five nights a week programme implies he said he would do it, so long as he could continue fronting Farming Diary and provided the executives in charge of the new magazine programme, to be called About Anglia, would agree to have at least one regular feature per week about agriculture. Dick was ahead of his time in realising the need to explain farming to an increasingly urbanised public. And since they were desperate to get Dick on the screen five nights a week, the executives had agreed. But they challenged Dick to come up with a formula to do what he wanted that would not cost the company too much and did not feature old farming fogies speaking unintelligible jargon that the average viewer would not understand. It needs to be pitched at about the same level as the radio soap, The Archers, they said.

Dick thought about it and decided the best place he could start was with the county's Young Farmers. He spoke first to Alf Milburn, the County Organiser and asked him to suggest a few names of possible candidates for the task Dick had in mind. Then he contacted Alf's relatively recent predecessor, Gordon Mosely, who had resigned from the YFC job when he had been head hunted by the BBC in Norwich to do VHF radio programmes for East Anglian farmers. Finally he consulted John Mann, the doyen of farm advisers in Norfolk and Chief County Officer for ADAS who was a regular attender at Young Farmers County meetings.

Each of these three compiled a short list of candidates based on their knowledge of the County's membership and mine, apparently, was the only name on all three lists. I suppose I was fairly high profile in YFC circles. I had a wife and a child which could potentially bring in a bit of family interest – just like in The Archers. And I'd recently taken on a new farm and was trying to make a go of it – which they probably thought might add a bit of drama. In any event, in the hope of short circuiting his search Dick decided to investigate the most favoured candidate first and that was me. And that's how he came to visit Whiterails and why I later went for the audition.

In the first instance I was booked for six live slots on consecutive Tuesday editions of About Anglia. In preparation for these the company stills photographer came out and took lots of still photographs of me, the livestock, and the farm buildings. Then a movie cameraman came and took some general shots around the farm to illustrate what I might say on the programme. And a day or two later one of the studio set builders arrived to measure the buildings from which he produced a scale model of the farmyard. It was only ever used a couple of times and then disappeared into the bowels of Anglia House. I never found out what happened to it despite enquiring because it would have been a marvellous keepsake that I would have loved to show my grandchildren. But I suspect it was thrown into the back of the storeroom and eventually got broken and discarded. The television industry, as I was to discover, is like that.

The day of my first broadcast arrived and I turned up at the studio in my best (and only) tweed sports jacket. Once again I was left in the Green Room until they were ready for a run-through in the studio. This was one of the two occasions on which the scale model of the farm was used and the entire six minutes was used to introduce me and the farm to viewers. Dick Joice interviewed me and asked me questions that were easy to answer because I was dealing with the subject matter I covered every day. And as I left the studio when my slot was over the producers PA handed me a wage envelope containing 7guineas (£7.7shillings or £7,35p). And that's how it was for each of the next five weeks during which Dick and I discussed pigs, beef cattle, autumn drilling of cereals, the family's involvement in the farm and sugar beet. I remember I took a few roots into the studio that day and explained that the sugar was in the juice and that they contained about 16% of sugar by weight. We weighed the root in the studio and I calculated that there would be enough sugar in that one root when processed to sweeten (and I've forgotten the figure) x cups of tea.

It was all pretty basic stuff and very much on a level with The Archers as the urban producers had demanded. And when I had done my sixth programme (and been handed my sixth wages envelope) I said to the producer well, that's my six slots. If you'd like me to come in again any time, let me know. "Oh David love", he said, "We want you to carry on coming in every Tuesday. Your items have become very popular you know. They bring a bit of fresh air into the studio. What are you going to tell us about next week?"

Needless to say I was rather pleased. I had started to get used to having a little more spending money and would have missed it. And so began a year long stint of doing weekly 6-minute slots every Tuesday. It was left to me what I decided to talk about each week and before long I found myself directing film camera's when they came out to the farm to film "wallpaper" for my part of the programme. One or two of the items we did starred Lorna. She was always a good cook and one week she demonstrated how to prepare and roast a guinea fowl. It was a few years pre-Delia Smith and perhaps the viewing public were not ready for cooking on the tele. If they had it could have been The Richardson's that ended up owning Norwich City Football Club.

On another occasion she spoke about the rabbits we hoped would make our fortune. I had heard about a fast-growing new breed of rabbit called a New Zealand White. Enthusiasts were suggesting at the time that they would compete with chicken and like them develop to become a staple for the table. Lorna was keen to try some and we bought a few does and a buck from Ray and Molly Page a husband and wife who owned an animal feed company and could supply the necessary pellets to feed them. We bought a supply of cages to keep them in and installed them in a disused chicken hut we'd inherited from the outgoing tenant. We also heard of another fast-growing breed that had been imported into this country from America called Californians. The first person to breed them in the UK was a man called Moss who lived near Tring in Hertfordshire. He turned out to be the father of Stirling Moss the racing driver and Lorna and I went down there one day a bought ten does and a buck of that breed to add to our rabbitry.

The Anglia producers were keen to feature this new enterprise in one of our Tuesday slots so Lorna took a few rabbits into the studio and described what we were trying to achieve. It went down well, apparently, attracting lots of interest from other potential rabbit farmers. But sadly the enterprise did not survive. The trouble with domesticated rabbits is that (unlike wild ones) they like dying too much. They're subject to a host of diseases and as soon as you put biggish numbers of them together the bugs breed faster than the rabbits. It was losses and vets bills that killed the concept and we didn't feel too silly to have tried it when we heard that Bernard Matthews had tried and failed with rabbits as well.

While all this was going on the politics of agriculture looked like it was about to change. Six nations across the Channel in Europe had begun to plan a Common Market and the British government, under Prime Minister, Harold Macmillan, was in talks to join them. This had the potential to change radically the system of support for farming in this country and the implications were huge.

As County Chairman of the Young Farmers I suggested we should hold a conference to discuss the matter and try to gain a better understanding of what might happen. We identified a lecturer at Reading University called Professor Hirsch and invited him to talk to a bunch of Norfolk members one Sunday at a hotel in Cromer. We were fascinated at what he told us and at the changes that would probably occur in this country if we joined. It was a really worthwhile day. But although I had invited a reporter from both the Eastern Daily Press, our county newspaper, and the East Anglian Farming World, also owned by Eastern Counties Newspapers and, rather obviously, targeted at farmers in the Eastern Counties, they had not turned up.

I was pretty fed up that such a useful conference would not get the publicity it deserved. So, the following Tuesday afternoon, between the rehearsal for my slot and the live programme, I marched down London Street in Norwich to the offices of Eastern Counties Newspapers and demanded to see the editor of the Farming World. Perhaps surprisingly I was ushered into his office and found myself face to face with this very gentle man, Bob Easter. "What is it you want to tell me, Mr Richardson," he said in his soft voice. And I did.

"I invited you to send a reporter to our conference last Sunday", I said, "and you couldn't be bothered. You report all the rubbish spouted at NFU county meetings but this was really valuable stuff and you missed it". And I went on to tell him what those of us there had learned. He sat through my rant and then said, "the trouble is, Mr Richardson, I would have had to pay a reporter in gold bars if I'd sent him to Cromer on a Sunday". But you seem to have a clear recollection of what was said.

Why don't you write 500 words on it for me? I could pay you 3guineas".

To say I was surprised would be an understatement. I had gone into his office full of aggression and to some extent criticised him personally only to be offered a job. Clearly it was a challenge I could not turn down and a couple of days later sent him the article. It was published in full the following week and the next day Bob Easter telephoned to say he liked the piece. Further, he said he'd been wondering how to cover Young Farmers affairs adequately in the magazine and he would like me to do 500 words on YFC's every week. He would pay 3 guineas for each article as he had for the first. Was I interested?

And so began another phase of my life that was to last even longer than television. At 23 I was a weekly columnist and it went on for about five years – until I felt I could no longer claim to be a Young Farmer. And once again I had been pushed in the deep end.

Chapter 11

Mixing the media and farming

Back home on the farm I was constantly looking for ways to make our operation more efficient and profitable. I investigated the possibility of growing different crops and pretty soon came up with the idea of trying vining peas and dwarf beans for freezing. Birds Eye had a processing factory at Great Yarmouth and some of my Young Farmer friends who farmed in East Norfolk were already growing for them. Indeed I'd grown a few broad beans for them myself – the ones my wife was weighing when Dick Joice called. The company was keen to expand and with nothing but the North Sea to the east of the factory (which had been built originally to make fish fingers from catches landed at Yarmouth and Lowestoft) it could only look west for more suppliers.

Enquiries revealed there were several farmers in our area who were also keen to try vining peas and we got together to form a co-operative to grow, harvest and deliver them to Birds Eye. It was a huge undertaking involving drilling the crops to a strict timetable so they ripened in that order and were able to be harvested in sequence and frozen while at their freshest and most tasty. That, anyway, was the theory. It worked most of the time but battling with unpredictable and variable weather and soil conditions it was not always possible to achieve the perfection Birds Eye demanded.

In those early days of harvesting peas for freezing there was a limited amount of mechanisation. First the crop had to be cut. It sounds simple when you say it quickly. But green peas have tendrils that wind around the stalks of their neighbours. When you cut one pea plant and try to move it you find it is connected directly or indirectly to dozens of others. So, we needed a cutting machine that could deal with that problem. The answer was a horizontal reciprocating knife that ran along close to the ground with further similar knives at each end set up at right angles in order to cut through those tendrils and leave a clean swathe of cut peas behind the machine.

Such machines were available, if a little crude, and had to be hydraulically mounted onto tractors. But the hydraulics and power drive on 1960's tractors were at the rear of the machines. Fifty years later front-end hydraulics and power sources are commonplace, but they weren't then. So, it was necessary to drive backwards to cut the peas. Various ingenious methods were invented, in farm workshops and elsewhere, to enable this to be done safely. They involved reversing the seat, relocating the steering wheel, the gear box, and the clutch, and making them all work conventionally as well for driving on the roads between fields and to enable the tractors to be used for other jobs when the pea harvest was over.

The worst job, however, was loading the cut swathe onto high sided lorries – a job that had to be done twenty-four hours a day to feed the factory and comply with the quality demands of Birds Eye. Green crop loaders had been invented by then to deal with grass silage for cattle feed and they were adapted to the task. They were sturdy machines, pulled and powered by tractors, that would pick up the heavy sappy material and elevate it to lorry height and drop it onto the floor of the vehicle. But in order to maximise the size of the load two men had to mount the lorry to "load" it – that is to say to move the green material around within the lorry with pitch forks to ensure the corners were all filled and to tread it until the lorry was at least level full.

It was hard and dangerous work, especially when the lorry was almost full and even more so through the hours of darkness with only tractor lights for illumination. And sometimes, when we had wet weather during July, it all had to happen during teeming rain with lorries getting stuck in mud in the middle of fields and having to be towed by yet more tractors. But the job had to continue so that the time that elapsed between the peas being mechanically removed from the pods and entering the freezing process twenty-five miles away was no more than ninety minutes. Yes, it was necessary to maintain the quality of the peas for consumers but I doubt if modern Health and Safety regulations would allow such a job to take place today – even if you could find men to do it, which I doubt.

These day's huge and expensive self-propelled vining machines separate the peas from the pods on the move on the field and tip the peas into lorry mounted stainless steel containers that still have to reach the factory within ninety minutes. It's still done through co-operatives with a number of growers sharing the capital costs and providing other machines and men. It's an altogether easier job for those who drive the machines although it can still be disrupted by wet weather.

Back in the 1960's I well remember my late father walking onto a field of our peas during the harvesting process. He looked at the number of tractors (often up to a dozen) and loaders (usually two or three) and lorries (sixteen to eighteen) and men (one for each tractor or lorry plus two to four loaders) involved, shook his head and said "I don't interfere with what you want to do and I know what a valuable crop peas are in the crop rotation giving us a good entry for winter wheat. But I cannot believe this circus can possibly be profitable".

He was right, of course, and fortunately the kind of mechanical developments pea growers now enjoy were not long coming. We stuck with the crop until that happened and along with others and with help from a government grant designed to encourage co-operative development invested in mobile vining machines. But once we'd invested Birds Eye clearly thought we were locked in on the crop and would grow peas whatever they paid us. The East Norfolk growers on their Grade 1 land could stand the financial pressure because they were able to grow consistently high yields. Meanwhile those of us on lower yielding Grade 111 land who were also further from the factory and therefore had higher transport costs began to realise we couldn't make vining peas pay and our co-operative disintegrated.

If all growers had stuck together and refused to grow unless we were offered a better price I'm confident Birds Eye would have succumbed. But although many said in grower's meetings that they would stick out for more money, when it came to the crunch they didn't. Indeed there was evidence that some who were especially committed to the crop for rotational reasons and because they could grow good yields would go straight from grower's meetings and phone Birds Eye to say that even if some farmers refused to grow they would pick up the spare acres and grow them on their land.

UK farmers are not good at co-operating or collective bargaining as I have since seen demonstrated on many occasions. But this was the first time I'd been so close to such behaviour and it disgusted me so much that we were the first to pull out of our local pea growing group. It didn't put me off co-operation for good as we shall see later but it did make me suspicious of some of my fellow farmers who, I realised, were too independent, not to say selfish, for their own, or the industry's good.

Meanwhile, my TV "career" continued. Having started my weekly appearances in the September of 1960, expecting them to end after six sessions, they carried on through the winter and the following spring and into summertime. Along the way the producers presumably gained confidence in me and it wasn't long before I was being used as "Mr Reliable" interviewee on whom they could try out greenhorn interviewers. Anglia was a very new station, remember, as was the whole ITV set-up and it sometimes felt as if the management was making it up as it went along.

One of the first of these try-out interviewers they foisted on me was a very tall young man, obviously straight out of university, who arrived in jeans and a pullover. But he had a beautiful "dark brown" broadcasting voice and the producers decided to give him a try. They fitted him up with jacket and trousers from wardrobe and sent him to me. He shook like a leaf before and during the live transmission and stuck like glue to the questions I had written out for him to ask me. It wasn't a great success but he did have a good voice and after a few sessions he took to the job fairly naturally. His name was Bob Wellings who went on to a long career with Anglia before moving to the BBC at Southampton and elsewhere.

Others who I was asked to "break in" that year included Dick Graham an ex-actor and natural broadcaster and mimic; Anne Gregg who later went to the BBC to do travel programmes among other things; Valerie Pitts who also later moved to the BBC for whom she was asked to interview the famous orchestral conductor, Sir Georg Solti whom she later married.

One Tuesday evening when I was in the studio another young interviewer appeared. He was a student at Cambridge and was trying to earn some money to fund him through university. He was a local boy and he'd been noticed in a Footlights review by one of the Anglia bigwigs who had invited him for a try out on *About Anglia*. I believe he'd done one or two interviews for the programme previously but I hadn't seen them (I still had no electricity or television set) and on this evening he was to interview Norfolk's Head of Education, Dr F Lincoln Ralphs about some aspect of the County's education system.

You have to understand that Dr Ralphs was a successful, long established not to say revered official in the County who probably sat at the right hand of God in his spare time. But that meant little to this young interviewer. He asked what, at that time, were regarded as impertinent questions and refused to accept the answers making even more impertinent follow-up comments. The entire studio was aghast including Dr Ralphs who, I suspect, complained bitterly to Anglia board members who were his contemporaries. You hear the same kind of interviews on The Today programme on Radio 4 and on Newsnight every day of the week these days. But back in 1961 interviewers were much more polite.

Needless to say that young interviewer never appeared on Anglia again. Which was a shame because his name was David Frost and he went on to make his name with the BBC on *That Was The Week That Was* and many other programmes. Many years later Lord Buxton, then Vice Chairman of Anglia Television, was apparently heard to say "A pity we lorst Frorst".

And so we came to the end of July 1961. It says a lot about the time and Anglia as a company operating in a rural area that they decided to give the nightly magazine programme, *About Anglia*, a few weeks off for harvest. As I left the studio after my last programme before the break the producer waved a cheery goodbye and said, "See you in September, David". To which I said thanks, but what did he want me to do in the new session. "Oh the same kinds of things you've done so well for us since last autumn, love", he replied. "But I've featured all the enterprises I have on my farm during the last year", I explained, "I don't think I can do them all again – can I?" "Oh, I hadn't realised that" he said, "can't you introduce some new ones to talk about next year?"

I explained that farming wasn't like that and he responded by saying that I was part of his plans for the following year and that I should go home and think how I could continue to bring farming into the programme each week and let him know. I had become used to earning my 7guineas each week and would miss it if it stopped so went home and did as he suggested. I was twenty-four with limited experience at broadcasting or anything else for that matter but I dared to wonder if I could become an interviewer. I had watched and assisted plenty during that first year and I had plenty of contacts, many made through Young Farmers, who did different things on their farms from what we did at home. I just might be able to stretch out a year's worth of weekly items by visiting them with a film crew or bringing them into the studio I thought – provided Anglia had enough faith in me to allow me to do it.

So I phoned the producer and suggested my ideas for the following year. He was ecstatic (but then he always was a bit over the top) and said it sounded wonderful. "But I don't have any spare staff to research these items", he said, "you'll have to do that and make all the arrangements. I think we could then pay you 10 guineas per item". Then he had an even better idea. "

"You know we now have an OB (outside broadcast) unit", he said. I did know because I had been involved with a programme that had used it on my farm earlier in the year. Mounted on a huge lorry, it had a single camera (and was nicknamed Cyclops for that reason) and wonder of wonders, featured a videotape recorder so that items could be recorded on location and played into the live programme when the tape was back at base. It took a crew of about a dozen people to operate it and had no editing facility so everything had to be recorded as live. But it was a major step forward for Anglia and for television.

"Why don't we send Cyclops out onto the farms you select so you can record them to insert into the programme?" the producer continued. "That way we can free up some studio space and bring some fresh air into the programme as well." He was a great one for fresh air in the studio although I doubt if he ever went out in it himself. He had little concept of what a muddy farmyard was like or what difficulties might occur as a result. But I had been offered the opportunity to continue earning a bit of much needed pocket money so accepted the challenge.

Each week I would contact one of my friends and invite myself to their farm to feature some aspect of what they were doing for the programme. The set-up for each had to be carefully thought out because of the limitations of only having one camera. In other words we had to virtually reproduce studio conditions outside on farms. This wasn't too difficult if we were doing an item on dairy cows, for instance, because they could be led out onto a field where I could talk about them to the farmer. I also persuaded another friend who owned a team of Percheron heavy horses to demonstrate their pulling power and how to control them. We did most of that piece while driving around a field to a predetermined course from the seat on his wagon, I remember. But the poultry farm I went to was a bit more of a problem because the hens were mostly inside big buildings and we had no lights. However, it was my job to come up with ideas on how we could record such items – all in one take – and most of them worked pretty well, at least for the standards and technology of the time.

To begin with the OB unit was allocated to me for a whole day for each item. The crew would turn up on the selected farm and in very leisurely fashion set up for the recording. There was a director to control the shots but otherwise I was not only the researcher but also interviewer and producer of the items. After a few weeks it became obvious to me that if properly planned it need not take all day to do a recording. Indeed it could easily be done in half a day. So I suggested to the boss that I could do two items per day if I arranged them to be close together to avoid a long journey between them. Once again, he was delighted. I was able to reduce the time spent on doing programmes to one day per fortnight (I did the research in the evenings so didn't count that time) and was able to earn two 10guinea fees for doing so.

I should make it clear that when I had negotiated to do the Outside Broadcasts I had been assured that the farmers I interviewed and whose farms and animals, etc, were used for the programmes would be paid the same as I was in nominal compensation for the disruption caused by having a dozen or so people and their vehicles on the farm, interfering with normal work. Indeed, when I persuaded people to allow me to feature their enterprises on the programme I always told them this was the case.

All went according to plan until one day in the summer of 1961 when I met, John Garner, a good friend, and fellow Young Farmer whose sheep and spring lambs I had featured a couple of months earlier. John wasn't one to beat about the bush. "I thought you said I'd get a cheque from Anglia for that programme we did", he said. "Nothing's turned up yet and it's about time I was paid." I apologised profusely and said I'd chase it up with the producer.

When I phoned him he was clearly embarrassed and said "Oh dear, David, love. I'm so sorry. Didn't anyone tell you? We've stopped paying outside contributors". Apparently the then executive director of the company, a man called Arthur Clifford, had decreed that this should happen but nobody had bothered to tell me.

I felt badly let down and incensed that I'd been made to look a fool and unreliable in the eyes of my friends. I phoned all those I could identify who had not been paid to apologise. And then walked into Arthur Clifford's office and told him what I thought of him. In retrospect it was a brave thing to do because he had a reputation for a nasty temper and was said, on one occasion, to have thrown a telephone out of a window. It was also rather arrogant of me to think such a man would bother much about a very junior contributor to his programmes but I felt morally obliged to have my say. Somewhat predictably he told me he could manage very well without my services (he wasn't quite that polite) and I was sacked. And that, I thought, was the end of my brief television career.

Chapter 12

BBC calling

I'd enjoyed my flirtation with TV – until it did the dirty on me that is – and I was still writing my YFC column for the *East Anglian Farming World*. But I missed the extra spending money and decided it was time to try to earn more out of the farm. Father and I discussed the possibilities and soon agreed that we should double the size of the pig breeding herd from 40 to 80 sows. Pigs had been a standby for him for years and I had earned my first money from them too. They were always "either copper or gold" as the saying went with profitability changing according to supply and demand. And because pigs can multiply quite fast – two litters of a dozen piglets per sow per year – that situation regularly changed every year or so. Farmers would breed their sows when times were good and stop breeding them when times were bad. But providing the production system was efficient and the pigs were well cared for it was usually possible to make a small margin, even during the bad periods and a better one when market demand improved. Bear in mind that this was in the days when most farmers kept a few pigs and stopping and starting was the norm. Today there are far fewer farmers keeping pigs and they all have much bigger numbers. They are therefore committed to production through thick and thin and the thin periods tend to last a lot longer.

But back in the early 1960's when there was a little less volatility we decided the gamble on pigs was worth taking. My close contacts with the people from ADAS helped confirm our decision. They confirmed that our financial performance with pigs was better than average and encouraged us to do what we wanted to do in any case. We owned a very small farm and a few acres in the village of Hethersett where both father and I had been raised and we set about building extra breeding and fattening pens to accommodate the additional sows and pigs. It was relatively quick to expand the number of sows. We just sent fewer gilt's (maiden females) to the bacon factory and a couple of months later put them to the boar. Four months later they had their first litters and six months after that those piglets were ready to slaughter for bacon. Our biggest challenge was keeping ahead of all this with the building programme.

Grandad Bowhill's building experience came into its own, as already indicated, we also employed a couple of freelance bricklayers from the village. It was a hectic but exciting time on the farm demanding total concentration and I was quite pleased not to have the distraction of having to leave to do television items. The arable side of the farm was developing too with the new land at Whiterails Farm looking a lot better for our management and growing heavier yielding crops than it had done for years. It was a very satisfying time. I was doing what I had always wanted to do since I was about eight years old. Lorna and I had a bouncing baby boy. The HP agreement for furniture had been paid off. We had a lovely house and a challenging farm to run. We weren't rich but we were happy.

One evening we were invited out to a yacht club dinner and dance by our friends Ray and Molly Page. Lorna and I had hardly ever been on a boat but Ray and Molly were keen sailors on the Norfolk Broads and asked us to go to the function as their guests. We hadn't been out much for some time so readily accepted. We arranged a babysitter for baby Andrew and set off for what was then called the Lido ballroom in Norwich. It was an enjoyable evening and after dinner we joined in the dancing.

As we circled the room I looked up and saw Gordon Mosley and his wife dancing nearby. Gordon, you will remember, had been the County Organiser of the Young Farmers before being head hunted to do radio programmes on farming by the BBC. He'd been one of the people who had recommended me to Dick Joice a couple of years earlier. Gordon saw me at the same time and when a few moments later our paths crossed he said, "I'm glad I've seen you," he said. "I was planning to phone you tomorrow". "Oh really", I replied, "What about?" By this time we'd both fetched up in a corner of the dance floor. "I was wondering if you'd like to do a bit of broadcasting for the BBC", he said. "I doubt it," I replied, thinking of my unfortunate departure from Anglia, "I don't much like the way broadcasting types exploit people and fail to keep their word. In any case I'm very busy at home on the farm and thoroughly enjoying it." Gordon said he understood and that in that case he'd have to look elsewhere. And we both danced off with our partners back to our tables.

As we sat down Lorna said, "Don't you think you'd better find out what he wants?" Later in the evening curiosity got the better of me too and I wandered across to where he was sitting with BBC Norwich's sports reporter, Ted Chamberlin. Gordon was not a sailor and like Lorna and me, he and his wife were guests of someone (Ted) who was.

"Perhaps you'd better tell me what it is you had in mind Gordon", I said rather sheepishly.

"Well," he said, "as you know I produce and present a weekly half hour regional radio programme called *For East Anglian Farmers*. But I've been invited by the Australian Broadcasting Corporation to spend six months in their country observing and advising on their farming programmes and I need someone to look after my radio programme while I'm away. I thought you might be interested".

I'd never done any radio before, as he well knew. But to gain time to consider what he'd said I told him this was the case. "But you've been doing television for a couple of years," he replied, "and radio is much easier." I hesitated again and pointed out that I'd only been doing five- or six-minute items and he was asking me to do half hour programmes. "That's right", he said, "and of course they are broadcast live." I asked him if he had anyone else in mind for the job to which he said he had not and that I was the right person to do it. Furthermore, that I would need to start two weeks later because that was when he was leaving for Australia.

"Look," he went on, "why don't you come into the studio next Wednesday afternoon and watch me do a programme to get the feel of it. You can meet my secretary, Betty, who'll be looking after you while I'm away. And you'll see – it'll be like falling off a log". By this time I was being carried along by his enthusiasm which was clearly influenced by his anxiety to get me in place in time to cover for his trip. I therefore agreed to go to BBC Norwich the following Wednesday but was still very uncertain whether I could or should do what Gordon wanted.

BBC Norwich had, a few years earlier, taken over a beautiful Georgian house close to the City centre. It had for a few years before that been an upmarket restaurant and I remember being taken there by a couple of aunts for afternoon tea when I was a child. It's since been converted into an upmarket dentist's surgery and a solicitor's office. But when I entered the grand front door there was the wide sweeping staircase in front of me just as I remembered it years earlier. Indeed it didn't look or feel a bit like a studio – at least not like the only one with which I was familiar just across the City where Anglia was based. That front hall was just like you'd expect in a well-appointed house, the only difference being a small discreet desk beside the staircase where the understated receptionist sat. There was a feeling that here was a national institution of long standing compared with the commercial, very new, and rather vulgar alternative down the road. Such comparisons would not hold good today but this was 1962 and Reithian principles still applied.

Gordon Mosley took me to his office, introduced me to his secretary Betty Bealey, and proceeded to explain what would be required of me. I would be responsible for deciding the topics to be discussed each week – usually up to five or six per programme – and the people to talk about them. I would travel out to farms or agricultural events, like shows, across East Anglia with a battery powered tape recorder (as big as a small suitcase) to interview individuals and the tapes could be played into the programme as required. I would invite people to the studio to be interviewed live on the programme. I would edit tapes with the help of in-house engineers. And, of course, I would present each programme at 6.15pm every Wednesday evening, making sure I finished precisely at 6.45pm to avoid crashing into the national transmission of *The Archers* which in those days began at that time.

"This is a huge job", I told Gordon, "and I'm not sure I can do it." Gordon, who was clearly panicking as his flight to Australia drew closer, told me not to worry and that Betty would help me with everything. But then I sat in the control room as Gordon presented that evening's programme. At the end of the programme as the time came closer to 6.45pm Gordon smoothly wrapped up the live interview he was conducting, busked a few words to fill the final seconds and bid listeners good evening just as *The Archers* was ready to start. Could I do that? I wondered. I had never been responsible for controlling a whole programme or the exact length of an item. Interviews I could do. But timing really worried me and I still hesitated to accept the job.

"Come in again next week", Gordon said, "and I'm sure you'll feel more familiar with it". So, to some extent against my better judgement, I agreed to do so. When I arrived the following Wednesday Gordon handed me a list of taped items to be included in that week's programme and told me a drainage expert was coming in to be interviewed live. "Why don't you look through these and write the script you'd use if you were presenting the programme?" he said, "then I'll have a look at it and tell you what I think." I did as he asked, writing it out longhand, and later handed it to him to check. "I can't read your scribble," he said.

"Betty, will you type this please so I can read it?"

Betty typed away for a while, managing to read my scribble perfectly well, and handed it to Gordon. He skimmed through it and said "This looks fine to me. I haven't written a script. The programme starts in half an hour. You'd better do the programme". And he put on his jacket and left the office.

Betty, who was clearly in on the subterfuge, calmed me down and reassured me that everything would be OK. She would be in the control room giving me any cue's I needed, she told me, and Oh yes, the interviewee whose drainage item would come last in the running order was waiting in reception. The next hour was a bit of a blur. I could hardly believe Gordon had just dumped the job in my lap but supposed I had better get on with it. I presented the programme, interviewed the drainage expert, and managed to wind-up on time. Betty told me I'd done alright. And Gordon later admitted he'd been sitting in the BBC car park listening to the programme just in case I messed up and he had to rush in and rescue me.

The following week he disappeared to Australia and I was in charge – with a lot of help from Betty. My training for the job really was as brief as I've described. The only other advice I received was from the Head of BBC Norwich, a professorial gentleman called David Bryson. "When you're doing interviews, old boy", he said, "Always try to preserve the balance of the argument". It was short and to the point but I've always tried to follow it – unlike many of today's broadcasters who can only function, it seems if they're campaigning about something. And that, by definition, means that the balance of the argument is not maintained. Times have changed and not necessarily for the better.

I found after a short while that I could do all that was required for *For East Anglian Farmers* in a day a week plus lots of phone calls from home, which was just as well because there was a lot to do on the farm. The pay was £20 per programme and we needed every penny because Lorna was pregnant again. But once again I had been pushed in at the deep end.

Chapter 13

Expanding activities in all directions

Our second son, Robert, quickly abbreviated to Rob, which he's been called ever since, was born in June 1962 at home on the farm. The bedroom in which it took place overlooked a field of green peas for freezing that we had just started growing. They were almost fit to harvest and therefore attractive to pigeons. I suggested to Lorna that she could make herself useful while recovering from the birth by shouting at the birds out of the window to frighten them away. Alternatively she could hold the baby, who was pretty noisy from the start, and hope his bawling did the trick. Needless to say my joke was not well received and I had to frighten the pigeons myself.

Around the same time a neighbouring farmer, also a tenant of the same estate from which we rented land, sadly died of Leukaemia. He was hardly middle aged and it was a great shock to everyone who knew him. Inevitably there was local speculation on who might be awarded the tenancy and I suspect several people were on the phone to the agent before the poor chap was cold. We decided not to join the queue of applicants. We were, after all, still consolidating after taking Whiterails Farm only four years previously and in any case we had too much respect for the deceased and his family.

Imagine our surprise when we received a phone call from the agent to ask if my father would be interested in the farm. The 270-acre holding was to be let without the farmhouse which the landlord wished to retain for use by his son who had recently married and was studying to be a barrister. My father already had his own house so was presumed not to need one and it was felt by the landowner, on the basis of his and perhaps my past record, that he would be the right person to take on the farm. Although this time I was specifically not to be included in the tenancy, obviously to enable the owner to regain possession when father died. But there would be no objection to us farming the land jointly like the land already rented from the estate we were told.

A lot of heart searching and another trip to the bank occupied our thoughts for the next few days ending with the conclusion agreed by all concerned that it was too good an opportunity to miss. And so, at Michaelmas 1962 father took the tenancy of Church Farm, Little Melton and we were farming around 700 acres. The landlords even agreed to grant father a long lease on a small field on the farm where he subsequently built a new house for mother and himself. They moved out of the house in the middle of the increasingly crowded village of Hethersett where they had lived all their married life and enjoyed nearly thirty years together surrounded by farmland.

Meanwhile, Gordon Mosley was still away and I was doing regular radio programmes for the BBC. It was a busy time and I had a number of discussions with father as to whether I should give up broadcasting. "You mustn't do that, "he said, "You never know what opportunities it might lead to." But I still felt guilty that when I was away and there was more pressure on him. "Don't worry", he said, "You catch up when you come back and I'm not complaining". I suspect, although he never said as much, that he derived vicarious pleasure from my media work and in any case encouraged me to accept any broadcasting invitations that came my way.

And before long they did. The first was from George Sigsworth, who was based at BBC HQ in Portland Place, London and was Head of Agricultural Programmes for the Corporation. He oversaw the output of the eight regional agricultural producers scattered around the country, of which I was now one, albeit the junior and temporary. The brief given to this team, all of whom had agricultural qualifications and/or experience was, through the weekly programmes they produced and presented, to inform and advise farmers in their areas how to manage their farms and produce more food more efficiently. It was, in a way, a hangover from the days of the Second World War, food shortages and ration books. Supplies of food were increasing every year and shortages were a thing of the past. But the Ministry of Agriculture was keen for the BBC to continue this service to the farming industry as an extension of educational activity for the ultimate benefit of consumers. Indeed, *The Archers*, that everyday story of country folk, still broadcast today but with very different story lines, was part of the same effort and came, loosely, under the same supervision as farming programmes rather than drama as might have been expected.

Among George Sigsworth's duties (he had, incidentally formerly been an adviser with the government's farm advisory service) he produced a weekly fifteen-minute radio programme on farming for The Third

Programme – now Radio 3. Not being a Radio 3 listener I'd never heard it. But a few weeks after I took over *For East Anglian Farmers* George rang to ask if I would do a two-minute piece for this programme. We'd never met but he introduced himself as a friend of Lorna's cousin, Willy Young, who had given Lorna away at our wedding, with whom he'd served the Ministry of Agriculture in Yorkshire. What a small world.

It transpired that every so often on his *Third Programme* show George did a roundup of farming conditions around the country. Information such as - whether work on the land was up to date; what was the weather like; how did the crops look; had livestock enough feed for the winter and so on. On that first occasion we'd been having very wet weather for too long and he asked each member of the farming team to record a short piece down the line to London on conditions in their area. All the others were staffers, of course, but I was a freelance and he offered me 8 guineas for the two minutes. "Is that OK?" he enquired. I replied that it was in as restrained a voice as I could manage and thought I was hitting the big time. It took me about fifteen minutes to write and record the piece and it was the best reward for time spent that I'd experienced to that point. I couldn't wait to be asked to do more.

BBC East Anglia had recently started its own regional TV magazine programme to compete with Anglia's early evening offering on which I had made my TV debut. One of the reporters on the programme was a gauche young man with a slight speech impediment in that he couldn't pronounce his r's called Graham Bell. His father, Adrian Bell, was a well-known writer on country matters, the author of several books and the compiler for many years of the Times crossword. But Graham was just beginning to establish a career in journalism which soon took him to London and on to some of the most dangerous War zones in the world, wearing the white suit that became his trademark. I have watched his career, including a short spell as an "honesty" MP, with interest and admiration ever since and recently met him again at a charity function in Norfolk at which he was speaking. We reminisced on those days long ago in Norwich with enormous pleasure.

It wasn't long before the producers of *Look East* were asking me to do pieces to camera on happenings in the countryside. The weather was an obvious subject and how it affected farming and might affect food prices. It was also a period when there was a fair bit of fowl pest around among the regions poultry flocks and I did a number of news items on the latest outbreaks of the disease. I soon became established as the regional farming expert and my "fame" spread.

Towards the end of my stint as Gordon Mosley's stand-in I received a phone call from John Kenyon, the producer of the BBC's national *Farming* programme broadcast from Birmingham each Sunday lunchtime. He'd heard about this young chap who was holding the fort in Norwich and wondered if I might be available to do the occasional filmed report for him. I said I would be pleased to do so, particularly since Gordon was due back any time and would resume his responsibilities. To my surprise I was immediately asked to go to Wrest Park at Silsoe in Bedfordshire where the now defunct National Institute of Agricultural Engineering was then situated. The Institute was about to launch a farm machinery testing scheme – a bit like an agricultural *Which* report on tractors and other tackle – and John wanted me to conduct interviews about it with some of the top people there for the Sunday programme.

A week or two later I found myself filming my first report for the national programme. I interviewed the Director of the Institute, a board member who claimed to be related to the founder of the world-famous Ransome ploughs, various engineering technicians and the film crew recorded the testing methods being used. The scheme was, I judged, essentially a good one even though the published reports were sometimes less than totally frank about problems because of pressure from manufacturers. Indeed that key problem was probably the main reason why it was abandoned a few years later. I tried to reflect these weaknesses in my report and a couple of weeks later the fifteen-minute item was broadcast.

As with the BBC radio programmes I had presented, the target audience was farmers rather than consumers or the general public and Sunday lunchtime is hardly a peak viewing period. We were farmers doing programmes for farmers and although we were aware of a substantial "over the shoulder" audience of viewers and listeners who may well have had farming forebears and who enjoyed seeing an industry at work, we did not set out to attract them. Today, programmes that feature farming, like *Countryfile* on BBC1 or the early morning radio programmes, are done by general reporters for consumers and as such are completely different and have become popular. Indeed I welcome the new style, particularly now they are sympathetic, in the main, to our industry's efforts, which was not always the case when the changes in emphasis were first made.

But the number of people who saw those first National TV programmes I did would have been measured in tens, or perhaps hundreds of thousands rather than millions. Even so, I took satisfaction from the fact that, aged 24 with virtually no training, qualifications, or university education, I had rubbed shoulders with and interviewed some of the top people in farm machinery and appeared on national television. And it didn't end there. Pretty soon there were other filming assignments which I happily fulfilled.

The Royal Norfolk Show was held, as usual that year at the end of June. I had been a junior steward of the Aberdeen Angus classes for a few years having been nominated by the Young Farmers office. But in 1962 I had to step down from that job because I had programme duties. Anthony Parkin, the BBC's senior regional agricultural producer based in Birmingham (which Norwich came under at the time as part of the Midland Region) had come over to Norfolk to keep an eye on me and help – or more accurately take over- production responsibilities for the show programme in which I still played a major part. After the programme went out the BBC gave a small party for participants. Any excuse was reason enough for a party as I was to learn.

Anthony, who I had met for the first time that day, got me in a corner and said he liked the way I broadcast and asked whether, once I was free of my Norwich involvement, I would be interested in helping him with his programme broadcast from Birmingham. "As you know," he said, "It's called *On Your Farm* and while up to now it's been a regional programme like the one you've been doing in Norwich, in the autumn it's going national on The Home Service (now Radio 4) and I'd like you to be my main presenter".

I told him I'd think about it and let him know. But I already knew I had to do it. I already knew that broadcasters' "lives" like professional footballers are usually pretty short. While your face and your voice fits, fine. But as soon as you're out of favour you're out of the door in no time. I decided I had better ride with the tide while it lasted and a few days later phoned to say I'd do it.

The biggest problem associated with presenting programmes from a studio in Birmingham was the distance from home. It was 174 miles door to door and neither the A14 nor the M6 had been built. Even on a good day it was a four hour journey each way and it took about another four hours to script and record *On Your Farm* each Friday. They were long days and I burned a lot of tyre rubber and petrol. But I loved doing the programme. Gordon Mosley had been right when he'd said radio was easier than television. In particular because there is so much less to go wrong, you're not relying on as many people to get their part in the production right all at the same time and in short it's easier to achieve what you set out to achieve. If that spells perfectionism, then I would have to admit to being a bit of a perfectionist.

I worked with Tony Parkin for about sixteen years on that programme and enjoyed almost every minute of it. He too was a perfectionist and was at times a hard task master. But behind the occasional tiff, we shared mutual respect and we did some memorable programmes together. A few other presenters were brought in from time to time to help with the weekly burden but I was pretty constant throughout the period. I shared studios with people I had idolised, like Ralph Whiteman who hailed from Piddletrenthide in Dorset. He had a fruity dark brown voice and an attractive west country accent and was a contemporary of Arthur (AG) Street whose columns I had read in *Farmers Weekly* for years but who I never met. Ralph was a lovely modest man despite his broadcasting longevity and to my amazement was much more nervous of the microphone than I was. He perspired so much during a broadcast that when he got up from the chair he would be dripping wet. But you'd never have guessed it from his delivery.

Preparing for one programme Tony played me a tape of a country girl reciting a poem she'd written entitled *I am a battery hen.* He'd been sent it by local radio Oxford who had broadcast it the previous week and the producer there wondered if we'd like to use it in *On Your Farm.* "What do you think?" asked Tony. "Can we use it on a serious programme like ours?" I replied that I thought it was hilarious and why shouldn't we include a bit of humour? So, that week we broadcast Pam Ayres for the first time on national radio and she went down a storm. Whatever happened to her?

One week when I was in Birmingham Tony said that he wanted to do occasional live outside broadcasts from farms in different parts of the country. Was I up for it? I said that I was and pretty soon we were doing them in our usual time slot of 7.15 on Saturday mornings once a month. We did a series of them from one farm for instance. It was on the edge of the Cotswolds and was owned and run by a lady called

Nancibel Gregory. She was a real character and nothing like as genteel as her name might suggest. She was a tough businesswoman who ran beef and sheep and some arable with a rod of iron. She also followed the local hunt and reared puppies for the kennels. We must have gone there half a dozen times one summer and enjoyed recording the seasons around the farm through the eyes of Nancibel, her nephew, her workers, her vet, and even on one occasion, her postman who, oblivious to the microphone, happened to deliver letters into her hand while Nancibel was broadcasting.

We travelled far and wide with the outside broadcasting (OB) unit for a few years including, on one occasion, to our farm in Norfolk when I had to swap roles and become an interviewee rather than an interviewer. Tony brought a couple of other interviewers to help with the programme and between the three of them they spoke to Lorna as she cooked breakfast, to me about the crops we were growing and the pigs, and to father about the single suckler herd of Blue Greys. Tony dealt with father as they leaned over a gate beside the water meadows.

As was his habit Tony set the scene. "I'm standing here in the middle of typical Norfolk countryside", he said, "And I'm looking at a herd of cattle that would probably be more at home in the hills of Scotland. They look to me like a cross between North Country Shorthorns and Aberdeen Angus. With me to tell me about them is Mr Robert Richardson, David's father. Mr Richardson, why are they here?"

"Well, they're here", said father, "because you asked me to move them onto this meadow so we could talk about them this morning, don't you remember?"

Father knew exactly what he was doing and took delight in teasing Tony, who really wanted to know why a Norfolk farm was running Scottish cattle. The answer was that we had a significant acreage of water meadows that were not suitable for arable cropping because they flooded in winter. They were too wet for sheep and probably harboured fluke. So hardy cattle like those we had bought in Scotland seemed the most appropriate.

But fathers' little joke, which had set Tony back on his heels, was one of the things that eventually persuaded him to give up live outside broadcasts. The other was the acute worry it caused him for hours before a transmission in case anything went wrong, and we lost the lines or a microphone went down. Fortunately, that only happened once and the continuity announcer in London had to play some music until we could make contact again. But Tony, the perfectionist, was psychologically unsuited to chaos and after a while began trying to think of other ways to reflect farming around the country rather than from a studio.

I think I can claim to have helped him find the answer. I had maintained my friendship with Dick Joice despite my unfortunate departure from Anglia. I had been asked by Norfolk Young Farmers to write, produce, and commentate a pageant for the Norfolk Show main ring programme and had decided to make it a satirical and hopefully amusing history of Norfolk agriculture with the title "Dew they don't now they did do". It had been suggested by fellow Young Farmer and wag, John Carrick and means, if you can translate from the Norfolk accent, "Even if people don't do such things these days they surely did in the past".

I needed to locate old horse drawn implements and other props for the Young Farmer "actors" to carry. I knew that one of Dick's hobbies was collecting such things (Later in his television career he presented a very popular programme called Bygones, often using items from his own extensive museum which is still on display at Holkham Hall).

I rang Dick and asked if he could help. "Corse I can, boy," he said, "You'd better come and see what I've got in the barn. Tell you what – why don't you come to breakfast next Saturday?" It was, I should make clear, becoming fashionable to hold breakfast meetings – a trend imported from America, chiefly by David Frost, who was, by this time famous for presenting *That Was The Week That Was*.

I was telling this story to Tony Parkin when we next met and suggested, instead of risking his first heart attack by doing more OB's on Saturday mornings, that we could visit farmers earlier in the week and record programmes, as live, over their breakfast tables which could then be transmitted in our usual slot. Tony didn't jump at the idea at first, but soon began promoting it as his own, and it wasn't long before breakfast programmes became a regular and very popular part of our schedule.

Chapter 14

Stress and recovery

Back on the farm the additional acres we were now farming meant we needed better machinery to handle grain as well as some means of drying it in case the weather was wet at harvest time and we were forced to combine at moisture levels unsuitable for storage or sale. Big, four-bushel corn sacks, open at the top, with thatching brotches (hazel sticks used to hold thatch in place on corn stacks, pronounced 'brortches' in Norfolk dialect) stuck down into the grain in the hope of releasing excess moisture would no longer be adequate, we concluded.

I began looking for a good second-hand tanker combine to replace our old bagging machine. Eventually I found a Claas Matador that I thought was suitable, a few years old and a little bit bigger than we really needed but it's a good feeling to be on top of the job and it wasn't too expensive because of its age. We'd been happy with our old Claas, especially the quick availability of spares, and we wanted to stick with a proven manufacturer. But the Matador was a bulk machine. That is to say it threshed the grain and delivered it to a tank on top to be augered into trailers running alongside rather than into sacks, thereby saving a great deal of backbreaking lifting.

We next had to arrange trailers that would take the grain off the combine and deliver it to store. We had a couple of three tonne OB Wright trailers on the farm already and decided to make demountable grain tanks to bolt onto them in the farm workshop. The tanks we made did us well for a few years. Today trailers that run alongside combines usually have a capacity of at least 15 tonnes to match the size and output of massive modern machines. But this was 1963 and we were as pleased as punch with what we had done.

However, the main challenge was to build a barn to store the grain. The traditional buildings at Whiterails Farm were only suitable for horse drawn implements or the equivalent size pulled by tractors and while they were perfectly OK for storing grain in sacks they were useless for bulk. We needed a new barn and some means to dry and condition the grain as well.

Contacts made while broadcasting had enabled me to keep in touch with the latest thinking on grain storage and I had heard of a development by Essex farmer and innovator, John Muirhead, that potentially would enable us to solve both the drying and the storage problem in one go. He had invented a system of ventilating grain through small A shaped ducts placed on the floor under a heap of grain and connected to a bigger tunnel through which air was blown under pressure. He had built such a store on his own farm and reports suggested it was successful.

I got together with the landlord's agent and my friends at NAAS, the governments advisory service and the forerunner of ADAS, and we planned our own version together. There were grants available to assist in the funding of projects of this kind and they helped a lot. We selected a suitable site behind the house in what used to be an extensive orchard that had run out of steam and the plan was afoot.

We decided to do some of the construction work with our own labour to save money. But I hadn't realised how long it would take. With harvest approaching fast in July 1963 we still had big sliding doors to make and fit and the pressure was intense. Freddie Collings, our workshop man and I did lots of 16-hour days at that time and went to bed exhausted every night. On top of that there was the worry as to whether the system would work as it was supposed to. We were, after all, almost pioneering. It was only the second grain store of its type that had ever been erected and we couldn't be absolutely sure.

To be honest, I was probably spreading myself too thinly. I was still fitting in a fair bit of broadcasting and writing and working hard physically as well. That combination of stresses added to tiredness was more than I should have subjected myself to and I suspect I came close to having a breakdown. But – we did get the building finished and it did work so I recovered quickly and have never felt myself as stressed since.

Indeed the building and the grain drying system attracted a lot of attention and we had a great many visits from farmers wanting to do something similar. Today it looks dated and old fashioned, for time has moved on. But then it was ground-breaking.

In the meantime I was invited to do more filmed stories for the BBC's Farming programme which took me all over the country. Each trip took two or three days and I learned an enormous amount, not only about the farms we filmed on but also the countryside through which I drove (at the BBC's expense) in order to do the job. The worst bit was driving to Birmingham and back in a day to write and record commentaries for the films. Sadly, these journeys seldom coincided with my *On Your Farm* radio commitments so I was soon clocking up considerable mileages.

Then I was asked to help present the studio element of the programme broadcast live on Sunday lunchtimes. This meant yet more journeys to Birmingham where, in those days, we used studio's at Gosta Green (a converted cinema) or Broad Street where the BBC had its Midlands headquarters. Both have since been demolished to make way for modern developments, and the last programmes I did from Birmingham were transmitted from the (then) new Pebble Mill studio. That too has now been replaced. But we made some memorable programmes in those often-cramped conditions and I was fast becoming a key member of the *Farming* team.

But I confess I was nervous when first asked to work alongside John Cherrington. He'd been my idol for years because of his television appearances and his weekly columns in the *Farmer & Stockbreeder* of fond memory. His knowledge of agriculture worldwide and his command of the politics of farming were legendary. He was unafraid of challenging anyone who's views he thought were faulty and he was at times feared but certainly respected by all who crossed his path. How would such a man react to a very junior and inexperienced person like me invading his territory, I wondered?

But I needn't have worried. A few days before my first scheduled live appearance he telephoned to suggest we had dinner together on the Saturday evening in the hotel in which we were both booked before doing the programme on Sunday morning. We were joined by his lovely wife, Ronnie (short for Veronica) and enjoyed a delightful evening. I was right that he wanted to find out all he could about me, and to establish my bona fides, and he asked me a great many questions. Growing in confidence as the evening progressed, I quizzed him too about the things I'd always wanted to know about him. By the end of the evening we had established the beginning of a warm friendship that lasted until he died.

But I suspect he still wanted to be sure about me and a few weeks later when we were together again he said "I believe you've got one of these new-fangled grain floor drying systems. Can I come over to Norfolk and have a look at it?" I said that, of course, he could and the following week, he and his youngest son arrived. We walked round the grain store and drove round the farm and then came in for lunch. Lorna had roasted a leg of lamb and all the trimmings, and I have never seen such trenchermen as Cherrington and Son. Lorna and I had a few slices but they consumed the rest. There was only a bone left for the dog. Whether it was Lorna's lunch or the farm that did it, I was given John's seal of approval that day.

It would be no exaggeration to suggest that he became my mentor and helped me in so many ways. My affection and respect for him grew and grew, and one day years later he let slip that he had looked up to Arthur (A.G.) Street, who wrote weekly articles in *Farmers Weekly* for many years as well as several books that became countryside classics, in much the same way I looked up to him.

These were the days of annual Farm Price Reviews each February when ministers of agriculture would announce the results of their negotiations with the NFU on the guaranteed prices of a range of farm commodities for the coming year. So important were these reviews – and our programme - that agriculture ministers were prepared to give up their Sundays to come to Birmingham to talk about what they had agreed.

On one occasion when Christopher Soames was Minister of Agriculture, he came into our Broad Street studio to say his piece. I was there that day to summarise the main measures in the package and John Cherrington was scheduled to talk to Soames about it afterwards. John and I were rehearsing the running order when the Minister arrived, and I stood quietly beside a panel on which the following year's prices were listed. John beckoned him over to sit in the chair beside him, but before sitting down Soames, having established which camera would be on him, reached into his pocket, fished out a £1 note (we still had them then), walked behind the said camera and thrust the note into the operator's hand saying "Keep the camera up as high as you can, old chap, I don't want my double chin to show". Little did he know the cameraman took direction from the gallery, not from politicians, however important and generous they might be.

Then he sat down beside John and asked, "How long have I got?" John checked the running order and replied, "It looks like about four minutes". At which Soames almost exploded. "How on earth do you think I can say all I want to say about my Price Review in four minutes?" he demanded.

This was not the first time John had found himself in such a situation with a politician, and John had a very effective put-down. He used it then on Christopher Soames. "May I remind you", he said, "that Abraham Lincoln defined democracy at Gettysburg (in the speech that talked about "government of the people, for the people, by the people") in one and a half minutes. If you can't speak about the most important aspects of your Price Review in four minutes – tough".

A few years later, Tony Parkin and I decided to do one of our radio breakfast programmes across the Cherrington's kitchen table. We travelled to Chute Standen near Andover in Hampshire and prepared in the usual way, turning up next morning to record the programme. We realised that, despite all his years of experience, John was really quite twitchy. In retrospect it was probably because this was all about him rather than other people or stories, and he wanted, very badly, to get it right.

The recording started; we asked a few questions about his early days, and John began reeling off anecdotes about his long life and experiences; about how he had walked out of a university course at Leeds after a few months, despite his banker father's wishes, when he concluded he was wasting his time; how he went to New Zealand (on which he later wrote a book entitled *On the Smell of an Oily Rag* referring to what a New Zealand sheep farmer had to live on when markets collapsed); the job he got feeding cattle on a ship as they were being delivered to Argentina; and so on.

Tony and I both realised that he was talking too much; that we were never going to get all the rest of his life story into the allotted half hour. After a bit, Tony stopped the tape and said, "Sorry John, but this isn't working". And he went on to explain the problem. John spluttered and said "Well you'll have to edit it. You told me you wanted these anecdotes and that's what you've got. Let's get on with the rest of it". Tony gently explained that he'd been so long winded that it wouldn't be possible to edit it to make sense. The only thing for it was to start again and keep the answers shorter. John exploded again – I'd never seen him in such a mood. At which point Ronnie, his wife, who had been sitting quietly during these exchanges put her hand on John's arm and said, "Remember Lincoln dear".

John wouldn't have taken it from anyone else, but Ronnie could handle him, and had said exactly the right thing. He realised he'd been trying too hard and gave in immediately. "Well, alright then," he said, "Let's have another cup of coffee and try it again. We did and it turned out to be one of the best "breakfasts" we ever broadcast.

One Sunday a few years later we were having lunch in the BBC canteen after doing the programme. One of the studio guests was Philip Hassall, an eminent journalist who at the time was taking a break from writing to be chief executive of The Grain and Feed Trade Association (Gafta) on which we'd just interviewed him. But he wasn't happy in the job and had been head hunted back into journalism. He was about to take over the editorship of a monthly controlled circulation magazine called *Farm & Country*, he told us with the intention of changing the title and the content to much more hard-hitting stuff centred around farm management. Under his editorship It later became *Big Farm Management*.

"I could do with a really good columnist" he said across the table, "I don't suppose I could persuade you to do one for me, John?" John replied that he couldn't walk out on the *Farmer & Stockbreeder*, he was already doing occasional pieces for the *Financial Times* (for whom he later became a weekly columnist) and he didn't think he wanted to do more. "In that case", Philip Hassall continued, "do you know anyone who could do it?"

"How about that young man across the table" said John nodding towards me to my absolute surprise. "Why don't you let him have a try?" Philip Hassall was as taken aback as I was and asked if I could write. I told him I'd written a column on Young Farmers for five years. To which Philip said "Well, that's a start". And before we parted half an hour later he said if John Cherrington thought I could do it I probably could. "Write a couple of 1,000-word pieces and send them to me" he said, "and I'll let you know if they're any good".

The following week I duly sent him the trial columns. He phoned back to say he like them both and would publish them. And out of the blue I had another freelance job writing monthly columns for *Farm & Country* which became *Big Farm Management* an arrangement that was to continue for about ten years.

One day in 1976, while I was still writing for *Big Farm Management*, Philip phoned. He told me that he was soon to launch a weekly controlled circulation magazine, to be called *Big Farm Weekly*, alongside the monthly and that he wanted me to write a weekly column for it. I told him I was flattered to be asked but that I didn't think I could sustain a weekly column. Get three other chaps and I'll do one a month for you, I said. But he wouldn't take no for an answer. "I know you can do it" he insisted. I continued to resist but eventually caved in but on my own terms. "I will do weekly columns for three months", I told him, "and at the end of that time if I am unhappy or you are unhappy we will both have the right to cancel the arrangement and revert to monthly pieces".

Suffice to say the three months passed and neither of us asked to cancel. I carried on until 1992 when farming was going through hard times and advertising became too thin to support *Big Farm Weekly* and it was sold to *Farmers Weekly*. At which point Stephen Howe, the FW's editor, invited me to transfer over to the new title and carried on almost as before. Forty years later I'm still writing regular columns for FW although not every week as I did originally. But I'm in danger of getting ahead of myself.

Primary school days. This was the whole school. I'm in the white shirt, backrow

Lorna and my father, Robert Richardson. Father had a fine bass voice and was often asked to sing. Lorna was a good pianist and accompanied him.

Part of Norwich Cattle (sheep) market in the late 1950's

Preparing to interview some pigs! First radio assignment for
BBC Norwich 1963. Photo BBC

Henry & Marjorie Plumb on their lawn in Coleshill,
Warwickshire when Henry was vice president of the NFU.
Henry later became an MEP and a peer

David and one of his blue-grey heifers bought at St Boswells market to graze the
water meadows at Whiterails Farm. 1960. Photo Anglia TV

David, his brother Philip and their father, Robert, when Farmers Weekly visited their farm prior to David's first paper at the Oxford Farming Conference. Photo Farmers Weekly

Recording an On Your Farm breakfast radio programme with Tony Parkin. He's the one on the right. Note the breakfast cereals and toast on the table. We really did eat breakfast as we recorded

Tasting Copella apple juice with Devora Peake the boss of the firm

With Dick Joice and some of my collection of pigs as we rehearsed for one of his Bygones programmes, for Anglia TV

My best (only) check jacket

The peasants were revolting! A photo I took from the steps of the European Parliament as agriculture was being debated inside. Later the riot police arrived and tear gassed the farmers. It was the first time I smelled tear gas - but not the last!

Sugar beet harvesting. An Anglia TV publicity photo

I'm the one on the left

Above and Below: Interviewing John Cherrington outside the old Ministry of Agriculture building in Whitehall Place, London

Myself when young

Me beside one of my beloved Claas combine harvesters

Farmers Weekly gives one of these every year. I got one in 2015

Lorna and me when I was President of the Royal Norfolk Show

Caroline Drummond, CEO of LEAF (Preface)

My family; left to right Andrew, Rob and Fiona

A publicity photo for Anglia TV

Relaxing by a field of sheep

Chapter 15

The son we nearly lost

Back in the early 1960's we were still consolidating our farming base. Money was still tight and I investigated every possible way to save expenditure. I set up a little workshop in one bay of an old cart shed, installed a vice, made a bench out of scrap metal and bought a second-hand electric welder at a farm auction for £37. That little workshop saved us a huge amount of money. We could do simple repair jobs without calling in mechanics from the local tractor repair business. And in the evenings I used the welding skills picked up when I was a student to weld spring steel onto worn out plough points to make them last twice as long.

After a while Freddie Collings, who I had made head tractor driver when the troublesome foreman left, hung around after work and started looking over my shoulder as I did these welding jobs. One evening I asked him if he'd like a go. "Yes please", he replied enthusiastically. And pretty soon he was a better welder than I was.

Freddie was a natural mechanic. But he was also very unsure of himself, mainly because he couldn't read. He was, I believe, a classic victim of dyslexia that had never been recognised when he was at school. He'd always been labelled as stupid and had come to believe it. But when I encouraged him his intelligence blossomed and he became our most valuable member of staff. He could construct anything with metal and a welding rod. He used to say to me "You draw it for me and I'll make it – you're better at the skull work". He took over the combine driving (although I still did mealtimes) and all the key tractor work as well as running the (by now) expanded workshop.

But although he had a licence to drive a tractor he didn't have one for a car, or van, which was becoming more important as his job expanded. I offered to treat him to lessons but for years he declined. We found out later that it was because he was frightened of being sent to Norwich, six miles away, to get spare parts or whatever, and being unable to find his way home - because he couldn't read the signs. Eventually I persuaded him that he must get his driving licence if he was to continue being as useful on the farm. He took the lessons and his instructor reported that he drove really well. But three times he failed his test because his inferiority complex took over and he went to pieces on the day.

I was determined we'd get him driving so insisted he try again. A few days before the fourth test he said, "I'm going to fail again, I know it". But this time I had a bright idea. I went to the local chemists' shop, run by an old school friend of mine, told him the story and asked if he could let me have a couple of tranquilisers. I'm afraid not, he said, but I can let you have a couple of coloured pills with nothing more sinister in them than iron supplement and you can tell your man what you want him to believe they will do for him. It might work.

I decided to give it a try. I knew that Freddie trusted me because of the way I'd enabled him to realise his potential and he'd do anything for me. So, the day before his fourth driving test I handed him the pills. "Freddie", I said, "You must take the blue one just before you go to bed tonight. It'll make you sleep like a top and you'll wake up tomorrow as fresh as a daisy. Then, an hour before the test, take the red pill. It'll keep you calm but alert for the next few hours by which time you'll have passed your test".

The following morning Freddie went off to the testing centre with a friend and just before lunch walked into the farmyard with a huge grin on his face. "Them pills worked" he said, "they done exactly what you said they'd do. And I've got my licence."

Several months later I told Freddie the truth about the pills. At first he wouldn't believe me. "But I slept soundly like you said I would and felt marvellous when I went for the test", he said. But he believed me in the end and realised that he'd passed on his own merits and not with the help of drugs. It was, however, the most dramatic example of successful auto suggestion I have ever experienced, and, I hope, contributed a bit more to building his self-confidence. Sadly, when he was in his mid-fifties he was sitting at home watching television one evening and had a massive heart attack and died. He was a good man and a great friend and I miss him still.

All through those years while my radio and television activities were expanding I still worked hard on the farm. If anything I worked longer hours when I was at home to try to compensate for my frequent absences. I did all the crop spraying, all the tractor hoeing of sugar beet, all the weighing of pigs to select which went off to the abattoir the following week and took my turn at feeding them, especially on those weekends when I wasn't in Birmingham in the studio. And I never accepted any invitations to go broadcasting during the month of August or early September when my priority was to supervise and work in the harvest.

Looking back, I suppose I was a bit of a workaholic. But I'd been reared to believe in the Protestant work ethic and having started in business with very little money I felt it wrong to turn down opportunities to earn a little more. And our living costs were increasing again, as Lorna became pregnant for the third time. This time it was a girl and we called her Fiona. When I went to see the pair of them after the birth in the Norfolk & Norwich hospital I took her a gramophone record as a present. It was of Maurice Chevalier singing the film classic "Thank heaven for little girls".

Between driving tractors and changing nappies (of which I did my share) I was travelling to Birmingham and around the country to film and do programmes with increasing regularity. I was getting to know many of the key characters in agriculture. One in particular, who was a rising star in the National Farmers Union, was a Warwickshire farmer called Henry Plumb. I'd heard him speak a few times at NFU AGM's and he was clearly someone to watch.

Then, in early 1965 he was elected to be Vice President of the Union at only 37 years old, which made him the youngest ever to hold that office at that time. He was a gift to both our radio and our television programmes, not only because of his youth but also because he lived and farmed just a few miles south of Birmingham. I first got to know him and his wife Marjorie properly when Tony Parkin and I did one of our outside broadcasts from his farm at Coleshill. At that time he ran a herd of two hundred Ayrshires, seventy breeding sows, and cropped the rest of his three hundred acres that wasn't growing fodder for cattle with cereals and potatoes.

He was very much a working farmer in those days milking his own cows and filling milk vending machines in the village to try to earn a premium price for some of it. He'd taken over the management of the farm when his father died very young several years earlier. And like me, he'd been noticed by those around him when he was a member of the Young Farmers Club. We hit it off immediately. He was about twelve years older than me but we had so much in common. And it wasn't long before I took to calling on Henry and Marjorie for a cup of tea occasionally on my way home from participating in a Sunday

Farming programme. It was an ideal opportunity for me to find out the latest NFU thinking on current issues and for Henry to elicit my first impressions. It was the beginning of a friendship that deepened over the years and survives to this day – through his election to the Presidency of the NFU in 1970, his election as a MEP in 1979, his Presidency of the European Parliament in 1987, the only Brit to do so, and his elevation to the Peerage in the same year.

In more recent years Henry has initiated a charitable Foundation to help young people involved in food and farming by providing them with cash and a mentor. I became a trustee of the Foundation and have derived enormous satisfaction from helping to select candidates many of whom have already begun to make their mark in the industry. As I write over 100 have so far benefited.

There were a few particularly interesting places to meet and talk to industry leaders and I soon began going to them regularly. The excuse was to report on them but I thoroughly enjoyed them anyway. The NFU AGM, held in those days at Central Hall Westminster was one. The Royal Show, at Stoneleigh Park, Warwickshire, now sadly no more, was another. The whole BBC farming team would attend it every year to produce reports for the following weekend's transmissions. And the Oxford Farming Conference, held among the dreaming spires of that university town each January was arguably best of all.

The annual Conference had been started back in the 1930's by forward looking, not to say pioneering farmers and the lecturers in agriculture at the University (where, sadly, they no longer run an agricultural course) and some of them were still (ageing) regulars in the early 1960's. Top speakers were invited from around the world as well as pre-eminent farmers, economists, and scientists from the UK. It was a rich source of academic and practical information and right from the start I found it stimulating. It was almost like attending the university I'd rejected years earlier but was now mature enough to appreciate. I've attended about fifty conferences since. Some years were better than others, of course, but once you get into the "Oxford habit" it's difficult to stop. I was there, initially, to interview speakers and contribute to reports on what had been said. But I was eventually, in 1982, elected to serve on the organising committee and in 1984 was Conference chairman, of which more later.

The 1966 Conference was a particularly inspiring one for me.

107

Speakers told, as they almost always do, how they were expanding their farming enterprises, improving their marketing, and overcoming difficulties. For some reason it got me fired up and I came home determined to follow some of those examples. I was convinced there was more we could achieve with our pigs and I set about working out how to expand the herd further.

One Sunday at the end of January 1966, a few weeks after that year's Oxford Conference, I was at home for a change. Someone else was presenting the Farming programme and I was sitting in the kitchen mulling over these half-formed plans and calculating likely costs and returns. It was a crisp cold morning and there was a layer of thin ice on the puddles in the yard. Ten months old Fiona was burbling in her pram and the two boys, Andrew, aged six and Rob aged three and a half, were out playing on the farm.

Suddenly Andrew burst into the kitchen shouting "Daddy, come quickly. Rob is drowning". Lorna, who was preparing Sunday lunch, and I, ran outside asking Andrew "Where is he?" Andrew pointed to where there was an old horse pond beside the drive. I had never run so fast in my life. When I got to the edge of the pond there was no sign of Rob. "Where is he?" I shouted again to Andrew who was following Lorna and I. "The other pond", he shouted back, pointing towards the one about a hundred yards further on across the front meadow.

As I sprinted towards that second pond I realised from the time it had taken for Andrew to run back to fetch us, that Rob must have been in the water for some minutes. And sure enough, when I reached the pond, I saw him head down in the water. He'd been kept afloat by air trapped in his little blue anorak, but his head and the rest of his body were under the surface and very still. I plunged down the steep bank where he had obviously slipped into the near freezing water. It was a deep part of the pond and I was up to my shoulders by the time I reached him. I grabbed his anorak and literally threw him up onto the bank.

A few days earlier I'd had to pull a calf out of one of our Blue Grey cows. The calf was stillborn – that's why she'd had difficulty delivering it on her own. As I threw Rob up onto the bank his little body felt just like that calf. I knew he was dead, and as I clambered up the bank out of the pond, I was paralysed with grief.

Lorna was cradling him on the ground and sobbing. And I suddenly had a flash of inspiration. A few days earlier I'd been waiting for another broadcaster from another programme to vacate a radio studio in Birmingham. I was annoyed because he was over-running his allotted time. I had stood there in the corridor outside the studio idly reading a first aid poster on the wall showing how to administer mouth to mouth resuscitation. I'd been awarded a first aid certificate in Young Farmers a few years earlier in training for which I had practiced the Holgar Nielsen method and the Schaffer methods of artificial respiration. But I'd never before seen information on how to do mouth to mouth. Instinctively I knew it was our only hope and I knelt down beside the little boy to see if it would work. "Go and phone the doctor," I said to Lorna, then set about trying to get Rob to breathe.

I blew into his mouth several times and gently pressed up and down on his tiny rib cage to try to stimulate his heart. Whether he had a pulse I can't say. My hands were too frozen to feel it in any case. After what seemed like a lifetime with no result I was about to give up. But I decided to try once more, and suddenly a gout of stomach contents and dirty pond water spewed out of his mouth and he gasped. I blew gently into his mouth a few more times and was rewarded with a few more gasps. By this time Lorna was back with a blanket which we wrapped around him and carried him back to the warm kitchen where he continued to gasp intermittently. A few minutes later Dr Stuart, our family GP, arrived from the next village. He pushed a tube down his throat into his lungs to keep his airway clear and ordered Lorna to cut off Rob's cold wet clothes. He was fantastic. He told me to get changed into some dry clothes – I'd been hardly conscious of my own condition - gave Lorna the telephone number of the local hospital and told her to ring and tell them he was on his way with an unconscious child.

Minutes later we set off in my car to the hospital. The doctor sat in the back seat holding Rob in a blanket and with a tube down his throat. The hospital staff were ready for the emergency and took charge telling me not to worry. And once Dr Stuart was satisfied Rob was in good hands he and I left and I drove him back to Whiterails and his car. "We must hope he wasn't under the water long enough to have caused brain damage", he said as I drove back. "But there's every hope he'll be OK".

A few hours later one of the nurses telephoned to say Rob had regained consciousness. I asked if I could collect him and bring him home and she replied that it would be best if he stayed in overnight so they could keep an eye on him. "But he seems OK" she said reassuringly. Early the next morning another nurse rang to ask when we could come and get Rob. "Is he alright?" we asked. "Oh yes," she replied, "He's climbing up the walls. Please come soon". That boy was always troublesome.

For weeks afterwards I would wake up in the middle of the night having relived the nightmare in my sleep. I'd get up and creep into Rob's bedroom to make sure he was breathing. Then I'd creep back to bed again trying not to wake Lorna. But she went through the same experience and once or twice we'd meet one another on the landing as we went to check him.

We could hardly believe how lucky we'd been. What if I hadn't been there that Sunday? What if I hadn't read that first aid poster a few days previously? What if Andrew, instead of coming to call us, had tried to pull Rob out of the water himself and fallen into the pond alongside him? What if the doctor had been out on another emergency call? There were so many "what ifs'". And it put all the thinking I'd been doing about expanding the farm and the pig herd into perspective. We decided the two most positive things we could do were, first to fence round the ponds on the front meadow – that was done the following week. And second, to teach the children to swim. Within a few days of the luckiest escape of our lives, we had booked Andrew and Rob weekly swimming lessons. Fiona was still too young, but we made sure she learned as soon as she was old enough.

Plans to expand the pigs were put on hold for a bit as we prioritised the children. I continued travelling backwards and forwards to Birmingham and other places to make programmes for the BBC but slowed down a bit to spend more time at home. Eventually we did expand both the pig herd and, from the extra profits they generated, the acreage we farmed. But we'd had a nasty shock that thank goodness turned out alright and it, perhaps necessarily, slowed us down.

Chapter 16

Back problems and hospitalisation

The decade of the 1960's saw farming margins coming under steadily increasing pressure. The food shortages of the War years and their aftermath were over. Ration books were becoming a distant memory. Subsidies paid to farmers to encourage greater food production so that British people didn't go hungry were being criticised. Farmers were accused of being "feather bedded" a phrase coined by Stanley Evans MP in the late 1950's that deliberately masked the fact that the ultimate beneficiaries of farm subsidies were consumers, because their existence helped hold down the cost of living. The truth was that as governments cut guaranteed prices and subsidies in response to public opinion it became a little harder each year to make a decent profit.

It was a trend that was to continue and, a few short periods apart, goes on to this day. How many consumers realise that the amount they spend on food these days represents only about 9% of average household income? The number of active farmers has gradually eroded as sons and daughters found easier ways to make a better living than their parents. The number of farm workers declined as well as wages increased and mechanisation took over many of their jobs. I well remember the words of "Uncle" Rob Alston, a wise old Scotsman who had come south in the 1930's and built a highly successful farming business in North East Norfolk. He and his wife, Belle, had no children and rather than leave his farm to his already well set up nieces and nephews he created and donated his farm to The Clan Trust, income from which still helps many young farmers and rural good causes in Norfolk.

As we stood next to one another at a shoot one day waiting for the beaters to drive the birds over us and discussing the state of farming he looked at me, a very junior member of the party, and said, "We need to put more horsepower under every man, David, it's the only way we're going to keep up with the pressure to cut food prices for consumers". At the time I was too young and inexperienced to realise how right he was. But I've thought of his words many times since and marvelled at his farsightedness.

Whether his words hold just as good forty years later is perhaps debateable. Tractors, trailers, combine harvesters, sugar beet harvesters and so on have become so huge and heavy in these early years of the twenty first century that I worry about the damage we are doing to soil structure. The economic arguments for enabling one man on a machine to do the work that dozens used to do still appear sound. But yields have plateaued in recent years following years of steady improvement. Plant breeders claim the genetic improvements they have bred into their varieties have continued. But the results, apart, perhaps, of sugar beet, have not come through to harvest and I seriously wonder if at least some of the reason is the way we've been treating, or rather mistreating, our soils. This has been widely recognised in recent years and is the subject of ongoing study. One possible solution is light robotic radio-controlled machines that are in their early stages of development. Meanwhile tractors and harvesters keep getting bigger.

However, back in the 1960's on our farm we were heavily into pigs. As already explained pigs have a reputation for cyclical returns, seldom holding their profitability more than a year or two before falling into losses. But we were fortunate, at the time, to have Fred Peart as Minister of Agriculture. He had entered parliament in the Labour Election victory in 1945 having previously been a teacher. But in that lean time after World War II he quickly became PPS to the then Minister of Agriculture, Tom Williams, the author two years later of the Agriculture Act of 1947 which was favourable to farmers and against which all subsequent agricultural legislation has been judged.

Fred Peart was obviously involved on the fringes of the negotiations that led to the 1947 Act and although not an intellectual giant, became friendly towards farmers. After the Labour Election victory of 1964 when Harold Wilson became Prime Minister, he asked Peart to be Minister of Agriculture and join the Cabinet. The new Minister brought with him the conviction that farmers needed stable incomes to produce the food the country needed and did all he could to provide them even as subsidies were cut.

Pigs were one of the most notoriously volatile sectors in farming so he set about dreaming up a scheme to help. What he, or more likely one of his advisers, came up with was a system that tracked the variation in pig numbers on a regular basis and if they increased by a predetermined percentage the guaranteed price of pig meat would be reduced to dampen producer's enthusiasm. If, on the other hand pig numbers fell, the guaranteed price would be raised to provide a signal that it was safe to build up numbers a little. Other factors like changes in the cost of pig feed were also taken into account but essentially it was a simple stabilisation scheme and it resulted in a longer period of price stability than the pig industry has ever known – before or since. It cost very little in that the governments contribution rose and fell alternately so in a way it was almost self-financing.

I've thought of that simple system many times since and how variations of it could be used to stabilise the prices and therefore the production of other farm commodities. But intervention is no longer fashionable. The market must rule according to economists. But the operation of supply and demand is similar in that prices and production go up and down – except that the swings are much more extreme and corrections take longer. Meanwhile consumers as well as producers suffer. In other words the market works but is too blunt an instrument for something as crucial as food supplies. A lighter touch, of the kind Fred Peart introduced for pigs, it seems to me, would suit all parties better. Indeed a similar system has, in recent years, been adopted for a range of farm commodities in the USA, so why is it not used in the UK too?

The thing is, the UK had a food policy during and immediately after the War, but we don't have one now. It's all left to the free market and in the hands of supermarkets which, between them supply 80% of all we eat. So it's no longer deemed necessary or affordable to employ civil servants to record production and likely demand. That means there is no evidence on which to base intervention even if ministers wanted to do so, and this is despite the worsening worldwide food crisis. In the meantime government sponsored organisations employ thousands to police how farmers look after the environment. It's not that I am against the environment. I'm very much in favour of environmental responsibility by farmers as will be seen later in this narrative. But it does seem to me that governments, led by the nose by single issue pressure groups that control a lot of votes, have distorted priorities.

And today's pig farmers get no help at all to level out their returns and haven't had since Fred Peart's day. The bigger herds, often kept outside, partly for slightly dubious welfare reasons but mainly because housing them is cheaper, have the effect of virtually forcing producers to try to ride out losses until they, or their bank, can't stand it anymore. Combine that with costly welfare standards, higher in the UK than in the rest of Europe, adopted unilaterally by this country and there were all the ingredients of a disaster waiting to happen. And sure enough in the ten or twelve years from the late 1990's to 2010 the UK pig population halved as producers gave up the struggle. And to satisfy consumer demand for pig meat Britain, or more accurately, British supermarkets, were forced to import from countries that used practices illegal here.

It was this kind of experience that motivated the NFU, supported by a host of other organisations, to insist that when Britain left the EU because of Brexit we must not allow imports of food that had been produced to lower standards than those that apply here. A lobbying campaign that attracted over a million Brit's to sign it virtually forced the government, to set up a Food Trade Commission to advise on food trade policy. The Commission came forward with many sound suggestions but it remains to be seen whether the Department of Trade takes any notice of them as it seeks to trade with the world.

But back in the 1960's we didn't realise how fortunate we were to be planning our modest further expansion in the days of relative stability. However, this was the time we decided to expand our pig herd again. We invested in more farrowing pens, weaner pools and fattening accommodation and pretty soon we joined the ranks of major producers. What was more – it was reasonably profitable for most of the time and we were able to build up some capital for the future expansion of the family farming enterprise.

This was becoming the new priority as we realised my younger brother, Philip, who was studying for a BScAgric at Reading University wanted to join us on the farm. He had always been more academic than me and for a number of years we had assumed he would choose to become a research scientist or something similar. But despite achieving a 1st Class Honours Degree in three years, rather than the normal four, he announced that he would like to join the family partnership.

We all agreed that it would be best if he did his own thing for a while to give himself time to confirm he'd made the right decision, and we managed to buy a fifty-acre farm set up to produce heavy hogs for Walls. We took over the farm as a going concern, and Philip moved into the farmhouse with his new wife, Julia. This time he was the one pushed in at the deep end, and for a few years he thrived on the hard work involved in producing pigs in rather worn and not very convenient buildings. It must have been a bit of a shock to his system after a life of unremitting study, but he stuck it and proved himself.

It was around this time, in the autumn of 1967, that an epidemic of Foot & Mouth disease struck Great Britain. Fortunately for those of us in the east, the epicentre was in the intensive dairying area of Cheshire, from where it spread to other counties. The speed the disease spread was unprecedented, with up to seventy new cases being reported on some days. Those of us involved with the BBC farming unit were torn between what we saw as our duty to inform farmers and the public on what was going on, and being ultra-careful not to spread it as we did so. I deemed it too risky to travel to the infected areas to report on cases and the measures being taken to try to control the situation, although I did continue my trips to the Birmingham studio's where we regularly featured aspects the disaster.

The organisers of The Smithfield Show, held annually at Earls Court in London during the first week in December in those days, debated whether to go ahead with the event. In the end they did, in order to provide a shop window for arable farming tackle, but no livestock were exhibited, and farmers with animals were discouraged from attending. I was there with a BBC film crew and we made a report of the most newsworthy features for the following Sunday's programme.

Meanwhile infected cattle sheep and pigs were being slaughtered and burned by the hundreds of thousands, causing misery to entire farming communities. Some of the finest and most irreplaceable herds and flocks in the country were lost. Rural life was disrupted for months; markets were unable to operate; hunting was banned; farm incomes were destroyed; people's lives were ruined. It was never established beyond doubt where the infection came from but circumstantial evidence pointed to frozen beef imported from Argentina.

There were investigations and reports written after the event to try to ensure such a tragedy never happened again. But, of course, it did. In 2001 the disease stuck again – this time, it is thought, because of infected swill fed to pigs. And once again the pyres burned thousands of animals on more than 2,000 farms where the disease struck in an epidemic that, once again, lasted many months. The total cost to the country of this latest outbreak was estimated at about £8billion. And still we allow meat from suspect sources to be imported through our ports without adequate inspection.

Political parties of all colours have let it be known that if there is another outbreak of Foot & Mouth in the future, government will not foot the bill for slaughter and compensation. Instead the farming industry will have to stand the losses. There would also probably be a vaccination programme instead of the slaughter policy – again funded by farmers. I suppose such changes are inevitable, given the huge costs, but given that infection can only reach these islands through ports and airports, and that these are manned by government inspectors whose job it is to stop infected products getting through, it is difficult to see the justice of making UK farmers not only the potential victims of a highly infectious animal disease, but also leaving them to face ruinous financial losses. We can only hope and pray it doesn't happen again. Although the Covid19 pandemic affecting humans, reminded me of those F&M days, and how passengers alighting from aircraft coming from infected countries were allowed to enter this country unchecked for many months. Will we never learn?

After the "excitement" of the 1967 Foot & Mouth epidemic – if that's the right description – the unaffected farmers of Britain quickly got back into their stride, as did the BBC. I had the privilege of working with various producers on some fascinating programmes. One series of three programmes that I particularly remember was about agricultural education. There were about thirty agricultural colleges across the country in those days and they offered different levels of education. Our series featured the whole range, starting with the supremely practical proficiency tests developed by the National Federation of Young Farmers Clubs and later adopted by the Agricultural Training Board. I had a few of those certificates hanging on my walls at home. Next we visited colleges where they ran courses for one to three years from which students could gain National Diploma's in Agriculture. And finally we went to universities, where the aim was to turn out Batchelors of Science or some equivalent in engineering or economics.

Having had minimal formal agricultural education myself, this exercise opened my eyes to what I had missed, and it wasn't all good. Yes, I had missed some of the scientific and economic stuff which I had to learn on the job, so to speak. I had also missed mixing for a few years with contemporaries on the same courses, and it took me a few years of mixing with the great and good of the industry to fill my address book with people I could call on for an objective opinion. But I was disappointed in the qualities of some of the lecturers. Some seemed to me to have stopped learning on the day they had qualified and never updated their views since. They knew little of the contemporary problems which I was battling every day, and as far as I could judge, did not read farming magazines nor watch or listen to farming programmes. Perhaps I judged all lecturers by the ones I met, and that may be unjust. But most of those I spoke to in making that series appeared to come into the category I have described.

Another series I presented was about water and the potential for shortage in the UK. It made me realise how precious our water supplies are, and how vulnerable we are to drought. Here in the UK we are among the most fortunate, being surrounded by water and having a marine climate. At least we do most years. But we use water far too carelessly, we don't collect it anything like as assiduously as we should, and we flush our toilets with purified product that should be reserved for more important things. We went to Wales and filmed the reservoirs there that serve the West Midlands. We went out on the Wash and speculated on how practical it would be to put a dam across from Lincolnshire to North Norfolk – a project the Dutch would have completed years before. And we studied ground water reserves across the country. We concluded that much more should be done to preserve our water resources and laid out a set of targets we thought the authorities should meet. That was back in the late 1960's, and I'm sad to say very little of what we envisaged has happened.

Another memorable filming trip was to the Hebrides – Skye and the Uists. We were away almost three weeks doing a number of stories about the crofter's simple but hard-working lives. We visited many of them to talk about their few acres of "inbye" land on which they grew oats and hay to feed their tiny herds and flocks through the winter. We went to the Tallisker whiskey distillery and tasted what they produced, got caught in a force 10gale crossing the notoriously rough seas called the Minch between Skye and North Uist, climbed (some of the way) up the Cullin mountain's, visited a woollen mill making pullovers, and so on. It was idyllic, peaceful, and relaxing. I took Lorna back there many years later to share the experience with her but it wasn't the same. The roads had been widened, the potholes filled, the ferry from the Scottish mainland had been replaced by a bridge. It was all so much more commercial – just like it is further south. But that's progress and it's unstoppable.

Back home on the farm our pig expansion was going well. The farm was profitable and the pigs were making a valuable contribution to the bottom line. Then my friend, Ray Page came to see me. It wasn't an unusual visit. We were using pig feed manufactured by his firm, Allen & Page based in Norwich so I assumed he wanted to talk about a price rise or something. It turned out that he wanted to expand his feed mill just as we were increasing our pig production. He felt there was a great deal of synergy between our two businesses and asked if I would become involved with his firm. I thought deeply about it for a few days before phoning him accepting his invitation and I have been a member of the Allen & Page board ever since.

In those early days we were trying to minimise the number of sacks of feed in favour of bulk handling – a repeat of what we had been through with grain handling on the farm some years before. And for a while this was a sound policy that saved costs all round. But several years later the UK's animal feed industry became even more competitive. Some of the big firms with household names, like Silcocks, Spillers, Bibbys and BOCM either disappeared or swallowed one another and margins became very tight.

By this time Ray Page's two sons had joined the business and they determined that it was time to change direction. We were not big enough to compete with the big national firms that fed most of the nation's pigs, cows, and chickens. Indeed some of them were not big enough to survive either. But there appeared to be a sizeable niche market providing specialist feeds for horses, back yard hens, miniature pigs, and so on. The boy's set-to to develop those areas of business and although Ray and I were a bit sceptical at first we were soon able to sit back and admire what they achieved.

They set up a national network of dealers (previously we had only been supplying farms in East Anglia); ditched all the bulk handling we had been using in the past, and supplied their products in illustrated paper bags, showing which classes of animals they were suitable for; and outsourced most of the transport, thereby cashing in on the competitive market that had made life difficult for us in the first place. It has been a wonderful example of success after embracing change. Had we stuck with feeding pigs we would have been bust long ago.

Early in 1970 one of our men, Eric Bell, biked into the farmyard early one morning and said, "I expect you've heard – Manor Farm Downham is up for sale". I wondered if it was pub talk because I hadn't heard anything. But he was in touch with the farmworker's grapevine, and he turned out to be right. For the record, the farm was in the next village to Great Melton, and some of the land joined Whiterails. Its owner was Dr Harold Hudson, (the doctorate was for science rather than medicine) whose main farm was a few miles away on the other side of our local town of Wymondham. He had bought Manor Farm for his daughter some years previously when she got married. It was common knowledge in the district that the marriage had been going through a rough patch so Eric's news had the ring of truth.

I knew Harold Hudson very well – mainly through Young Farmers of which he was a keen supporter. So after breakfast I phoned him to ask if the rumour was true. He was slightly taken aback that I'd heard the information before he'd wanted it to get out. But he was friendly and helpful when I told him I would be interested if he did decide to sell. "Why don't you come round for coffee later this morning", he said, "and I'd be grateful if you'd keep the situation private for the time being".

It emerged that he was pretty fed up, not to say embarrassed, at the breakdown of his daughter's marriage and was keen to sell the farm as quickly and quietly as possible. He was a bit of a fan of what I was doing in broadcasting and writing and couldn't have been happier that I had been the first person on the phone to enquire about the farm.

It extended to 270 acres, had a really nice Tudor farmhouse, recently renovated, together with four good cottages. The land type was very similar to what we were already farming, and it was next door. We conducted the negotiations discreetly as Harold Hudson requested, and within days we had agreed terms for taking over the place the following Michaelmas. It was exactly what we wanted and we considered ourselves fortunate. It brought the acreage we were farming up to 1,400.

As a family we decided it would be appropriate for my brother Philip to live in the house. The tenancy agreement on Whiterails Farm stated that I must reside there otherwise I might have been tempted. But it enabled Philip to move from the small pig farm he'd been running for a couple of years, into much better accommodation, and we appointed a manager to take his place. Philip was then able to take a fuller role in the arable farming as well as continue his interest in pigs. And the fact that he was now closer to the core of the business freed me up to carry on broadcasting which was to become more important for reasons of my health.

My back, injured when I lifted all those heavy sacks of grain when I was in my late teens, was causing me more and more problems. The fact that I was still working hard physically to compensate for my absences just made it worse. And during the harvest of that year it almost let me down altogether and I was of less and less use on the farm.

I decided something needed to be done about it and got an appointment with a local orthopaedic surgeon and friend, Ian Taylor. After he had X-rayed and examined me, he sat me down and said he didn't think I was a suitable candidate for a disc replacement or removal, but that I should benefit from a few weeks on permanent traction. A bed was booked at the Norfolk and Norwich hospital, and in September 1970 I began the most boring three-and-a-half-weeks of my life: in a hospital bed, the foot of which had been lifted up on blocks to be about 9 inches higher than the head. Around my ankles, bandages were wound, and wide strips of Elastoplast stretched from under those bandages past my feet to two small pulley wheels on which wire ropes ran. At the end of each wire rope was a lead weight containing enough metal to add up to eight pounds.

And there I was imprisoned. I couldn't get out of bed. I couldn't turn over. I just had to lie there on my back with my head nine inches lower than my feet. Indeed I remember a visit from our family solicitor while I was there. He needed the final signatures to complete the purchase of Manor Farm and they couldn't wait. If you've ever tried writing with your pen upside down you'll be able to imagine how difficult it was. But I managed it somehow, and the purchase went through as planned.

But Mr Taylor, the back specialist, held my attention when he came to see me before I was released from the hospital. "You need to take on board the probability, if you continue to work as hard physically," he said, "that you'll be in a wheelchair in less than five years". I was thirty-three and I don't mind admitting the prospect frightened me.

When, some weeks later, I began to recover from the traction torture, I called at BBC Norwich and for the first and only time in my life asked if they had any freelance broadcasting jobs going. It so happened that they were looking for a presenter for the daily TV magazine programme, *Look East*. Thinking it would be a lot easier sitting in front of a TV camera behind a desk than unloading lorry loads of pig feed and fertiliser I jumped at the chance and for the next two years alternated, week and week about, with Suzanne Hall, fitting in my continuing programmes from Birmingham during my week off *Look East*. On a magazine programme like *Look East* you never know who you might be asked to interview or what subject you might have to speak about. That period certainly broadened my mind. Among many other things I found myself introducing items by a young lady who came into the studio who was just starting a TV cooking career. Her name was Delia Smith.

I did lots of other jobs for BBC Norwich at that time while my back was recovering, including the occasional stint as a radio disc-jockey – well a mixture of music and recorded pieces from around the region anyway. On one occasion when the regular newsreader was ill, I even read the radio news and announced the football results. And it was this local exposure that led my old mucker Gordon Mosley to invite me to present a new monthly TV programme he was planning about the East Anglian countryside.

Chapter 17

Loddon Farmer's co-operative

Through the 1960's as memories of food rationing became more distant and farming profits more difficult to achieve the encouragement of co-operation between farmers became "politically correct", although that phrase was not introduced until much later. The Ministry of Agriculture decided to offer generous grants to groups of farmers who agreed to work together. These were not simply handouts to grasping farmers but attempts to improve efficiency and hold down the cost of food production and by implication, the cost of living and inflation.

Our pea growing group, for instance, had benefited from such grants when we purchased new harvesting equipment to replace our old labour-intensive tackle. Indeed it would have been difficult to have raised the capital to purchase the new machines without the grants. Although it soon became clear that the processing company for whom we grew the peas thought they should benefit as well and they squeezed our margins relentlessly.

The grant scheme was administered for the government by a Quango, another word that had not been invented at the time but that's what it was, entitled The Central Council for Agricultural and Horticultural Co-operation. It employed evangelistic experts who travelled the country advising farmers how co-ops should be set up. And, in tune with the times, I had conducted countless interviews with the directors of such bodies for both TV and radio programmes. The trouble was that the rate of failure of farm co-ops was alarmingly high.

Time after time we would feature on our programmes co-operatives designed to enable groups of farmers to jointly produce and market beef, or pigs, or crops of different kinds, only to hear six months or a year later that it had collapsed. We British farmers are notoriously independent and are not good co-operators.

Across most of Europe, farmers co-operatives have been much more successful, probably because most of the farms on the Continent were, and remain, much smaller than they are in Britain. The Code Napoleon, which applied over much of Europe, dictated that on every death, land should be divided equally between the offspring of the deceased. The result was tiny unprofitable blocks of land that were unviable unless their owners worked together. In Britain, inheritance laws had been different since the Middle Ages, and although these could legitimately have been argued to favour the eldest son they did, at least, maintain viable parcels of land, rather than splitting them into smaller and smaller bits every generation. But that in turn fed the desire for independence and to a lack of enthusiasm to co-operate.

There were, of course, notable exceptions to what I have described, and a few of those co-ops formed back in the 1960's went on to become very successful businesses that still exist and thrive today. But although I have no reliable statistics to prove it, my belief is that there were far more failures than successes.

All of which meant that I had an innate suspicion of co-ops, and did not keep my feelings to myself. We had joined one requisite co-op, Loddon Farmers, that operated locally because we believed it could, by virtue of bulk ordering, save us money on our farm inputs. But we did not get involved with any marketing groups because, in my broadcasting experience, they were the ones most likely to go under.

So, it was somewhat surprising to me when, in 1972, Colin Rackham, the Chief Executive of Loddon Farmers, contacted me to invite me to stand for election to his board. I explained my reservations which came as no surprise to him. He said he shared my opinions in many respects and that he wanted board members who questioned the more outlandish ideas of enthusiasts and brought a hard-headed business-like attitude to the job. He assured me that Loddon Farmers under his management would only act as a supplier of other company's goods at discounted prices, and not diversify into marketing. Indeed, he told me the existing board had already hived off a potato marketing idea that had been brought to it. That initiative became Anglian Produce, which, after several high-profile years also failed.

Eventually Colin persuaded me to allow my name to go forward for election to the Loddon board. I doubted that I would be elected because of my well-known reservations. But I was wrong and a few weeks later found myself sitting at the board table. My old YFC friend and skiing mate, Gavin Paterson sat opposite me and we looked at one another, and then at some of the others around the table. I've forgotten if it was him or me who asked "How long have you lot been on the board?" The answer was that some of them had been there since the company was initiated. Wouldn't it be a good idea to bring in some fresh ideas? We asked. And there and then we devised a system that allowed each board member to be elected for three terms of three years at which point they must stand down. If, after a year off the board, members chose to re-elect them they could be nominated for another similar period.

I had no way of knowing at the time that after I had served my first nine years on the board and then come off it, I would be nominated again and serve a further nine years. That was certainly not my intention when we proposed restricting the period that could be served. But I suppose I was the exception that proved the rule. In most walks of life, and with most positions I have held I have observed my own belief that nine or ten years is enough; that it is then time to step aside for people with new ideas that may be better than mine.

When I joined the Loddon board in 1972 the turnover was about £750,000. When I left it in 1991 for the second and last time it was approaching £25million. Inflation accounted for a fair bit of that, of course, but the rest was increased trade from a growing membership which presumably thought we were doing a decent job. We never did diversify into marketing, although we did start a training group, and began to provide agronomy services. But we were obsessive and successful in holding down the costs of administration to below 1%.

During my years on the board, of which thirteen were as chairman, we negotiated what I believe were the first retrospective discounts for farm inputs on the basis of the volume of trade. The deal was done with ICI fertilisers, and Colin Rackham and I travelled to their headquarters at Billingham a few times to close it. The same principles that we and ICI pioneered have been copied or varied many times since with a variety of products, but we were pleased to have made the breakthrough.

One of our initiatives that was not successful was to effect a merger between Loddon Farmers and Mid Norfolk Farmers. It seemed to Colin and I that there was a natural fit between the two groups that would cut costs, increase turnover and therefore discounts, and benefit members. But although the boards of both co-ops appeared to be in favour, there was resistance from the staff which we were unable to overcome.

My successor in the Loddon chair, John Andrews, tried again a few years later but came up against similar problems, and again the idea was aborted. But by the time James Alston took the Loddon chair times had started to change. Some of the top executives in both co-ops were getting ready to retire, and the boards of both were still enthusiastic to join together. A few months later the merger between Loddon and Mid Norfolk was announced under the new name Anglia Farmers ,which has gone on to merge with several other groups to become the biggest farmer's co-operative in Britain. Now a nationwide business it has renamed itself AF, presumably to disguise the fact that they are based near Norwich. But they have continued the policy of sticking to supplies for farms and not ventured into marketing. The co-operative appears to be going from strength to strength.

Chapter 18

We join the Common Market

The 1970's saw increasing world-wide public interest in the countryside – much of it unfavourable to farming. Books were written by ardent conservationists such as Marion Shoard condemning many new farming practices, not least the use of chemical sprays. The organic farming movement that had been pretty well under the public radar began to attract more adherents. And people whose parents or grandparents had historically worked on the land but who had themselves moved away from the country into jobs in towns became nostalgic for their past and sought to satisfy that nostalgia by criticising those of us producing food in new ways.

In addition, in this decade during which Britain eventually joined the Common Market, Europe's intervention system of agricultural support provided significantly better returns for farmers than they had recently been used to despite a couple of years – 1975 and 1976 – when there were crop yield sapping droughts. Towards the end of the decade when Margaret Thatcher came to power, and Peter Walker became Minister of Agriculture, he launched a campaign to maximise home production of food.

The good commodity prices guaranteed by the Common Market system, combined with overt government support, encouraged increased production of almost every commodity that could be produced on British farms. It also encouraged innovative ideas, and scientists brought forward concepts that had been gestating for years. For instance, researchers suggested that splitting top dressings of nitrogen fertilisers into three applications on wheat during the spring and summer, rather than applying it in one go in the early spring, as had been commonplace in the past, would increase yields. Other researchers revealed that they had successfully controlled some leaf diseases on wheat and barley by spraying them a few times during the growing season with solutions containing sulphur.

Forward looking farmers, including ourselves, were quick to try the new ideas, and thrilled to find they worked. I was invited to give the opening paper at the national Power Farming Conference in Bournemouth in the late 1970's and chose to concentrate on these emerging technologies. I pointed out that travelling through crops several times during the year with tractors and machines of different widths was in danger of damaging many plants and cancelling most of the benefits the fertilisers and sprays might deliver. What was needed, I said from the platform, was for an integrated system to be developed whereby tractors, fertiliser spreaders and sprayers could use the same tracks for each operation – if you like, I added," tramlines" through the crops.

I discovered later that my ideas were not new – that in other parts of Europe farmers had already started using "wheelways" across their cereal fields. But I claim to have invented the term tramlines to describe what we needed in Britain, and it has been used here ever since. What a shame I didn't copyright it.

Plant breeders also had a hand in increasing yields by bringing forward new varieties of cereals that responded to the techniques being developed. Chief among these was Norfolk man John Bingham who became, arguably, the most successful British wheat breeder ever from his base at the Plant Breeding Institute in Cambridge. He and his colleagues launched a stream of new varieties with the Maris prefix (so named after the lane on which the Institute was located). And the combined effect of all these new technologies was to significantly increase production, to the point that after a few years, Europe's intervention stores were full and consumers and governments began to question the practice of guaranteeing prices for commodities "which nobody wanted".

This too generated criticism by the media, egged on by extreme conservationists, but the actions of a few farmers who could not tolerate what they saw as interference in their legitimate businesses added to public disquiet about what some thought we were all doing. One such farmer was Hughie Batchelor who was a very successful Kentish farmer. To improve his efficiency still further, he cut down lots of trees, despite preservation orders, and demolished hedges between fields so his machines had fewer interruptions during cultivations and harvesting. Batchelor was so determined to continue such practices that he ended up in court and, probably because he refused to show any remorse, was sent to prison for contempt.

Needless to say most farmers were more attuned to changing public opinion and were prepared to modify their behaviour. But Hughie

Batchelor was not entirely without support from some older farmers who remembered being ordered to cut down trees and remove hedges during the Second World War as part of the emergency measures designed to feed the nation during hostilities. The difference was that during the War there were acute shortages. By the end of the 1970's Britain's farmers were starting to produce too much, and the surpluses were an embarrassment.

It was while this scenario was developing that Gordon Mosley asked if I would be the presenter of a new monthly countryside TV programme he was hoping to launch in the East Anglian region. It would include items on nature and these would be by Ted Ellis, the doyen of nature columnists in the local paper, the *Eastern Daily Press*; visits to bird sanctuaries, items on rural crafts, farm diversifications that were unusual at the time, and any other topics we thought might be interesting to the viewing audience.

I recognised this as an opportunity to reach some of the critics of farming, realising that I as a farmer would be able to help interpret some of the things going-on on farms while presenting countryside stories. It was a subject I was becoming passionate about so I accepted with enthusiasm, and Gordon and I worked happily together on the programme for a few years. It was, I suppose, like a regional *Countryfile* as we know it today, except that unlike Adam Henson, I didn't have a farm full of rare breeds of livestock.

When I look back now, I sometimes wonder how I fitted in all my farming and media activities. I was doing more each year for BBC *Farming* TV including driving to and from Birmingham most Sundays to present the programme. I filmed items on farms all over the country for the same programme on a regular basis, occasionally travelling to London, Brussels or Strasbourg to interview agriculture ministers or NFU office holders. I was the main presenter of *On Your Farm*, the Saturday morning radio programme, also put together in Birmingham but the schedules seldom matched so I had to make special journeys to do it. And I was writing a weekly column for *Big Farm Weekly*. Oh yes, and I was helping to run a 1,400-acre mixed farm and hold my family together. I was extremely fortunate to have a father and a brother as partners who were happy to allow me to fulfil all these engagements, and a wife who tolerated my absences and held the family together.

Then one Sunday when John Cherrington and I were doing a TV

Farming programme together, he took me to one side and asked if I would be prepared to write an occasional column for the *Financial Times*. By this time John had become established as the weekly farming columnist on the *FT*'s Commodities page. But he did not feel confident writing about sugar beet, vining peas and other East Anglian crops, nor did he know much about pigs. Busy as I was I knew I had to accept and so began a series of occasional columns which appeared on Tuesdays in Cherrington's slot. The arrangement went on for several years until, when John died just a couple of days after writing his final piece, the editor invited me to replace him, which, after a decent interval, I did.

I did ten years as main farming columnist at the *FT* before a new Editor decided that food was less important than metals to his worldwide readership and asked me to step down. Like most other people he looked at the surpluses farmers were producing and decided farming didn't matter anymore. He filled the space with news of the price and availability of copper, zinc and lead, which was I suppose, of interest to several of his readers. I did point out to him during the conversation when he sacked me, that food was of interest to all his readers. But he said I couldn't make that argument stick, and that as the paper was published in several centres around the world, I was underestimating how important metals were in the paper.

I couldn't complain too much. The FT treated me well during my ten-year stint and I received regular mail from around the world from readers of my columns – more than from any other media in which I have been involved. And it was probably the most prestigious job I ever did. But I did suggest to the Editor that the time would come when food supplies and self-sufficiency would be top of the news again. And I suspect I am about to be proved right.

The amount of driving I was doing during this period of intense activity was huge. Forty thousand miles a year was normal, and a high proportion of it was between home in Norfolk and the various studios in Birmingham. I came to know every bend in that road by heart, so much so that I didn't have to think about the journey. I was on automatic pilot. But it got to the stage when I would suddenly "wake up", not that I was asleep, but clearly not concentrating, and realise I was in Bedford or Northampton, or somewhere else along the route. This was before the A14 was built, and cross country was the only route to take. I never had an accident but I did become paranoid that what I was doing was unsafe and it worried me.

While these fears played on my mind, I received a phone call from Colin Ewing of Anglia TV who had succeeded Dick Joice and one or two others in between in producing the weekly *Farming Diary* TV programme and by this time had become Deputy Programme Controller for Anglia TV. *Farming Diary* was the Eastern regions main competition to the BBC's *Farming* which I had been involved with for 16 years, and it was produced in Norwich. Colin asked if he could come and see me and when he did he offered me the job of *Farming Diary* presenter. He knew of the other country programmes I was doing for BBC Norwich and said he'd like me to do something similar. I reminded him of my previous experience with Anglia, but he reassured me that things were very different now. He mentioned a fee that sounded quite attractive. But what really swung it for me was that the Norwich studio was eight miles from home compared with Birmingham's 174 miles.

I said I would let him know in a day or two to give myself time to think it over. But I knew it was right to accept, partly because of my personal safety when driving but also because *Farming Diary* was recorded each Friday rather than done live on Sundays. This meant I would spend a fraction of my time on the road and also have the whole of each weekend free to be with my family – and spend more time on the farm. So, with the proviso that I would continue to do programmes for BBC radio, mainly those recorded over breakfast tables, I accepted Anglia's offer and a few weeks later began presenting *Farming Diary*.

Chapter 19

Itchy feet

The 2nd World War, petrol rationing and our family's modest income meant that travelling was limited while I was a child. Journeys from our home in Hethersett were restricted, in the main, to trips to see the cattle on the Acle marshes, near Yarmouth, weekly visits to Norwich livestock market and after the War, an occasional journey further afield to visit friends and relations in other parts of the country.

One trip, I remember, was to a village called Cudworth in County Durham, where my mother and father had friends. I was ten and my brother was still a baby in a carry-cot. We went to see some of our friends' friend's, and memorably had the privilege of going down a coal mine with an official they knew well. At my tender age this was a fantastic adventure. I remember being fitted with a helmet with a light on the front and a boiler suit that was far too big for me. We climbed into the lift to take us down into the bowels of the earth and it went so fast I felt I had left my stomach on the surface.

Once down to the level at which coal was being hewn from the rock, our guide said he wanted to let us experience real darkness. He switched off our head lamps and suddenly we could almost feel the darkness it was so black. I don't and never have suffered from claustrophobia, but that was as near as I ever came to it. We switched our lights back on again and walked along gangways towards the coal face dodging trucks filled with coal travelling on narrow railway lines coming the other way. Mines weren't mechanised then as they later became and when we eventually reached the miners we found them bent double with picks in hand hacking lumps of coal from a face about four feet high. How those men tolerated such conditions day after day I shall never know. Our guide assured us that they got used to it, and often found it difficult to adapt to a new coalface of a different height.

Retracing our steps towards the bottom of the shaft we passed the "stables" where pit ponies were kept. There were dozens of them and they spent their entire lives underground. Apparently they knew their way round the mine, and once the trucks they pulled were loaded, they were given a slap on the rump and told to deliver their load to the collection point where the truck was emptied and they were sent back to the face to pick up another load. The ponies were well looked after and in good condition, but I could understand when old age meant they had to be retired and sent to the surface that it would take them a while to get used to daylight. I don't think ponies are used in Britain's depleted number of mines these days, and I am glad. It was no life for a sentient animal.

Another of our visits on that trip north was to a grocer's shop run by another of our host's friends. In fact it was to wish the grocer and his wife goodbye as we had met them before and we were about to head back to Norfolk. Ushering us into his storeroom at the back of the shop so as not to interrupt customers the grocer wished us goodbye and a safe journey back. But as we turned to leave, father noticed in a corner a pile of bags of sugar with Cantley Sugar Factory stencilled on them. "Well, would you believe it", he said, "I might have grown some of that". For Cantley was the factory to which we send our sugar beet for processing. Bear in mind that at that time, in 1947, sugar was still strictly rationed.

"Then let me give you a bag to take home", said the grocer. To which mother said no we couldn't possibly. It was too generous and in any case would be illegal. But father thought it was too good an opportunity to miss and to mother's embarrassment said thank you very much. A hundredweight bag of sugar was carried out of the shop and placed flat along the back seat of the car. My brother's carry-cot was placed on top of it along with all manner of blankets and other masking material and we set off for home.

Each time we passed a policeman on the long journey I thought mother would have kittens. She urged father to drive carefully so as not to attract the attention of the authorities. Mother was a very law-abiding person. So was father, but he was also a pragmatist.

When we arrived home the sugar was surreptitiously carried into the farmhouse and hidden in a cupboard in an upstairs bedroom. And every time mother wanted some sugar out of the bag I was told to check out of the bedroom window that nobody was coming down the drive. She was so relieved when the sugar was all used that I wondered if it had all been worth it. Father just grinned and said it would have been a shame not to have consumed some of what might have been our own produce.

A year later when petrol rationing had eased slightly, I went with my parents to Scotland and saw my first real mountains, lochs, and waterfalls. I wrote an essay on the trip when we got back, and described distant sheep on the hills as looking "a bit like rabbits tails among the heather". My primary school teacher was impressed at my observation, and I got top marks.

A few years later when I was thirteen and attending the City of Norwich Grammar School I had the opportunity to join a school party to Switzerland during a school holiday. The cost was £33 and I had saved up more than that from my pig keeping activities, so paying for it was not a problem. The trip was to be supervised by teachers, so it didn't take long for my parents to agree to let me go. We travelled by coach to Harwich, where we boarded the ferry to the Hook of Holland. There we boarded a train which took us on the long journey across Holland, through Germany to Lucerne in Switzerland.

This was not long after the tragic January floods that had overwhelmed large areas of Holland and drowned many hundreds of people. The same storms had wrought havoc along the Norfolk coast as well, but there were fewer casualties. I remember looking out of the train windows and seeing water marks halfway up houses, realising this was the level the floods had reached just a few months previously.

Later on our train ride we went through German towns that had obviously been devastated by Allied bombs a few years previously, although perhaps it was as well that night fell and darkness prevented us from seeing more of the devastation of war. Next morning we arrived at the beautiful City of Lucerne, and we travelled along the edge of Lake Lucerne to stay in a Gasthof (guesthouse or pub) in the pretty village of Brunen overlooking the Lake. I don't have many clear memories of what we did, except the pillow fights in our dormitory bedrooms. But I do remember my appreciation of snow-capped mountains and making up my mind to see as much of this beautiful world as possible.

A few years later I joined another school trip to Austria where we stayed in a small village called Axams, not far from Innsbruck. I had fallen in love with mountains which contrasted with our relatively flat land in East Anglia. Like the trip to Switzerland, this was in summer, so there was no skiing. But I resolved that as soon as I could afford it I would come back to try out this fantastically exciting looking sport whose popularity had only just started to build. But that was still many years into the future.

The next opportunity I had to travel was through Young Farmers. The National Federation of YFC's organised, and still organise, extended overseas travel for selected members. Those members are called Ambassadors and are expected to live and work on host farms in the country of their choice, benefiting from the cultural exchange, and improving relations between nations. When I was rising twenty I had held a few offices in my local club and served on the County Executive Committee, and I decided to put myself forward for a six-month exchange visit to Canada.

I was interviewed by County officials and then sent forward to Cambridge for possible regional selection. I was interviewed and asked to wait for a while as the adjudicators decided between the various candidates. I knew there were at least two others who had put in for Canada. Eventually I was asked back into the interview room and told I had not been selected, not because I was unsuitable, but because one of the other candidates was a few years older than me and they thought I could try again the following year.

Three months later I heard I had been given the tenancy of Whiterails Farm. There was no way I could contemplate leaving the farm for six months the following year, so that, it appeared at the time, would be the end of my travelling, and I would just have to control my itchy feet. I had no idea that within a few years I would be presenting TV and radio programmes, some of which would take me all over Europe and beyond.

But Young Farmers had not quite finished with me. I became the Norfolk representative on the National Federations Council, which meant travelling to London for meetings at YFC HQ – 55 Gower Street - and elsewhere a few times a year. The lady there who was in charge of exchange visits was called Barbara Tylden and she took a shine to me. One day at a meeting in London she asked if I would consider leading a study tour to Holland. There would be 20 Young Farmers plus me. The tour was to be sponsored by Vicon, the Dutch hay turner manufacturer, and based in the village where their factory was situated called Nieuw Vennep, quite close to Amsterdam, and almost adjacent to Schiphol Airport.

By this time I was married with one son almost two years old, with another child on the way. I really had to have approval from Lorna as well as my father before I said yes. They reasoned that as it was only a ten-day tour that they could manage without me, so I accepted the invitation.

The party met at Southend Airport, where there was a grass runway at the time. Our transport to Holland was an old Dakota bomber that had survived the War and been converted for passengers. I had never flown before, and nor had most of the Young Farmers party. So it was with some trepidation that we boarded the aircraft for the hour-long flight to Rotterdam. We soon felt we knew how the Battle of Britain flyers felt as the plane bounced along the makeshift runway. The trouble was it kept bouncing once we were airborne, as we went through air pockets on the low level flight. Needless to say nothing untoward happened and the old plane was probably as safe as houses. It was just that most of the passengers were inexperienced and didn't know what to expect.

Our host in Holland was a Vicon employee called Piet Vogelaar – his surname meant bird catcher – who was also a local farmer's son. He took us on a wonderful tour of his small country, explaining that one third of it was below sea level. We visited arable and livestock farms; we saw the famous clock auction for flowers; we went to the famous Flevohof, or kitchen garden, where acres of colourful tulips were in full bloom; and we learned how the Dutch had mastered the control of water. We soon picked up the fact that situated at the mouth of The Rhine river, with the big port of Rotterdam leading out to the North Sea, the Dutch had established themselves as a key trading nation for the whole of Europe. Virtually everyone spoke at least three languages – Dutch, German, and English – and trading was clearly second nature to them.

This was best illustrated when Piet took me to see his father's farm. It was only 120-acres, but it was all alluvial soil, and capable of growing excellent crops of potatoes, sugar beet and wheat. Piet took me into the "Dutch" coverall barn where the machinery was kept. I soon felt slightly superior in management terms for here was this "smallholder" with three tractors, a combine harvester, a sugar beet harvester, a potato harvester, a sprayer, and goodness knows what else. In British terms he was seriously over capitalised with machinery, even though most of it was a few years old. But I held my tongue which was just as well. Because when we went into the farmhouse for a cup of coffee the old man began discussing with Piet his concerns for a weather delayed cargo ship of maize that he had bought from the USA and which he intended trading to Dutch animal feed manufacturers once it arrived in Rotterdam. I had underestimated this old man who I had assumed was just a poor farmer like many in the UK. And he was typical of many others I met on that tour.

135

Another memorable tour took place in 1973. It was a press trip to the USA to look at "no-till" farming funded by ICI, one of the biggest forces in British agriculture at the time, but whose star has now sadly dimmed. It was my first trip across the Atlantic. Arranged by Ian Allen for ICI, it was intended to show us assembled hacks what the chemical Gramoxone – a contact killer of all green growth - could achieve in controlling weeds and cheapening cultivations. In the USA it was also used to kill surface weeds and avoid disturbing the soil so that it stayed relatively stable and did not erode during intense rainstorms. It was the first time I was to see "no-till" farming. Tony Parkin, who was also on the trip, and I did many interviews on that subject for *On Your Farm* and in those terms it was very productive.

But our tour, in July 1973, coincided with a US/European farm crisis to do with soya beans. Jimmy Carter, who was US President at the time, had imposed an export embargo on the beans, and Europe was panicking at running short of animal protein to include in pig and poultry rations. Petrus Lardinois, the Commissioner for Agriculture for the Common Market, had flown to Washington DC at almost the same time we had, and was giving press conferences for all media people who would listen. Ian Allen managed to get us invited to the Washington Press Club where he was speaking, and we were able to report on one of the hottest farm stories of the moment – an unexpected bonus on top of what was already a good trip.

For very different, and not as happy reasons, a trip to Spain for Anglia TV in 1978 was also memorable. It was not long after I had joined the company to take over much of the presenting of *Farming Diary*. Spain was in process of joining the Common Market. Our researcher, David Sawday, had gone ahead to set up farmers to visit and people to interview and the producer, Bill Smith, the film crew and I were to follow a week or so later.

I had been concerned about my mother for some weeks. Throughout her life she had suffered with poor health particularly with stomach trouble. She probably had a stomach ulcer, but the drugs to treat such a condition had not yet been developed. Now she had a more serious problem. She had been in and out of hospital with something the medics called aplastic anaemia. Blood transfusions helped her to feel better, but after a few weeks she deteriorated and had to have another.

One evening when I went into the hospital to see her, I had decided to cancel the trip to Spain and someone else would have to replace me in front of the camera. But the first thing she said when I sat down beside her bed was "When are you going to Spain?" I started to tell her I was not going because I needed to be at home with her as ill as she was. "Don't be silly", she said, "Of course you must go. I'll still be here when you get back." I tried to argue with her but she would have none of it, saying she would worry more if I didn't go and do my job.

It was an impossible dilemma which was only resolved when my father also said I should go to Spain, and that he would keep me in touch with mother's condition every day by phone.

So off we went, the film crew and I, to the sweeping plains of Southern Spain, with its huge fields of dry land wheat and bright yellow sunflowers, whose blooms turned to face the sun wherever it was in the sky. For a week we took some fantastic film under a hot sun. We interviewed a local aristocratic landowner called El Conde de la Maza (Conde means Count) who was also Mayor of the local town – Moron de la Fronterra. He grew wheat and sunflowers and had extensive drip irrigated orchards. He rode a motor bike; kept a string of fantastic Argentinian polo ponies; and his hobby was breeding fighting bulls, whose mothers he "performance" tested himself in his own small arena. In other words he was a larger-than-life character and it was a privilege to get to know him.

Each evening when we returned to our hotel I would phone home to check on mother. Reports to that point had indicated she was holding her own, until one evening when I rang I was appalled to learn that she had passed away. I was filled with grief and guilt at not being there for her and flew home as early as possible the next day leaving the film crew to get their final shots. I don't suppose I could have done anything to have changed things even if I had been at home but my absence at that time has haunted me ever since. When she died Mother was just 66.

In the months leading to her death, and well before she had gone to hospital she had been in need of constant care. Father had, by this time, turned over the management of the farm to my brother and myself, so spent a great deal of his time at home to respond to her needs. The rest of the family made frequent visits to see how mother was, and I had begun to notice on some of my visits that father was spending a lot of time writing at the kitchen table. "What are you writing", I enquired. "Well", he replied, "you've been telling me for years that I should write down all the stories and anecdotes that have become family folklore. I haven't been able to do anything else with your mother upstairs in bed, so I've been filling my time doing what you asked".

And he handed me a sheaf of handwritten pages on all kinds of paper from the backs of old calendars to discarded circular letters. Clearly writing down these anecdotes had become a sort of therapy for him as he worried about mother. And he hadn't finished. The scraps of paper kept on coming. At the time we had the luxury of a secretary in the office and without reading fathers "manuscripts" I laid them on her desk as I collected them and asked her to type them.

Some weeks later she asked me if I had read what she had typed. I replied that I had been too busy. To which she said she thought I should because there was some "entertaining stuff" in what he had written and it might be worth publishing. I took her at her word and made the effort. And very soon I agreed with her. It was autobiographical, but rather disorganised and would clearly need some editing, "cutting and pasting" and some gaps in the narrative would need to be written. But I decided to investigate the possibility of producing a book, maybe not for sale but mainly for the interest of our extended family.

Only three miles away, in the town of Wymondham, was a small printing company run by an old friend of the family, Brian Seager. I went to see him and told him what I had in mind and asked what it would cost to print, say, a hundred copies of a book written by father. "Why restrict it to a hundred", he said, "I know your father and I'm sure it will be a good read, and you won't have any problem selling a thousand. And I can print that number for less than half the price per copy that I would have to charge you for a hundred."

He'd persuaded me, and so began an intense period of editing and designing father's book. Much midnight oil was burned as I fitted it in between my other commitments. I told father I was going to publish his stories and that the book would be for general sale. I also listed further sections I would like him to write to complete the project. Suddenly he became self-conscious. All the stuff he had written to that point was chatty and easy reading. But as soon as he realised it might go further than family, he started using long words and adopted a more stilted style. Indeed I had to re write the last bits of the copy to make it match all the rest.

I looked out a few old family photographs to include in the book, asked my eldest son, Andrew, to draw some cartoons to illustrate events for which there were no photo's, and put my mind to thinking of a title. The book, as it had now become, recorded things that had gone wrong in father's life as well as things that had gone right. There were also a couple of chapters about the religious beliefs that had guided him. It therefore seemed appropriate to call it "*Some Fell on Stony Ground*".

We published towards the end of 1978, and I persuaded some of my media friends to review it. Without exception they were very kind – either that or they really did enjoy it – and 1000 copies went on sale. Three weeks later they had all gone and I had to order a reprint of another 1000. They took a little longer to move but I eventually ordered a second reprint and most of them sold quite fast as well. Bearing in mind that the average sale of books was said to be about 1,500 copies I took some satisfaction that my first publishing venture had been successful. Father was legitimately even more proud and we donated all the profits from sales to the Methodist Church at Hethersett where he worshipped all his life.

This chapter began with discussion about travelling which I have enjoyed since I was a boy and later became a fascinating theme running through my life. What I did not expect as the decade of the 1970's ended and the 1980's began, was that I was about to be given the opportunity to travel further than ever before. An old friend I had known since my days as a Young Farmer contacted me to see if I would be interested in leading a study tour of agriculture to China. Her name was Jill Lewis, and with a colleague called Bob Martin (no connection with dog medicines), had started and developed a specialist farming travel agency called The Agricultural Travel Bureau. It's still operating from offices in Newark with the new name of Field Farm Tours. At the time she was looking for someone to help plan foreign tours, to be a bit of a figure head when marketing them and to help organise visits and any speeches that had to be made while on the tours.

It was too good an opportunity to miss, and Jill made it clear that my wife, Lorna, would be able to join me, which I knew she would love. We went on that first tour to China and took about thirty farmers and their wives or partners with us. It was a few years after the Cultural Revolution and it was a real eye opener. We've been back twice since – once in 1999 and then again in 2008 – and the changes over that period were almost unbelievable. At least in the cities they were. Out in the country the farming had not changed much at all. Farmers still ploughed their tiny paddy fields with oxen, and scraped a living from the soil, in contrast to the enormous wealth that has been accumulated by some urban entrepreneurs. Will this inequality eventually lead to another revolution? Who knows?

After that first tour, Jill invited us to take groups to Australia, New Zealand, South Africa, Zimbabwe, Zambia, Japan, Russia, The USA, Canada, various countries in South America, Morocco, Cuba, Egypt and the Middle East, Turkey, and all over Europe – some of them a few times - and Lorna was able to be with me on most of them. We have been privileged to learn at first-hand how farming works in those countries and to have visited farmers and their wives in their homes. We have also made close and lasting friendships with fellow UK travellers.

When I think back to my disappointment at not being awarded a YFC scholarship to Canada and the prospect, as I believed at the time, that I would be stuck at home for the rest of my life, I count myself very lucky indeed.

Chapter 20

Travelling for fun

The money I earned from my off-farm activities was never as big as some might imagine. I was not doing programmes that attracted millions of listeners or viewers, nor writing for publications with millions of readers. My cheques were measured in ten's and sometimes a few hundreds of pounds, not the thousands that real show business performers could attract. Furthermore the "extras" that are available to most of today's "talent" were denied to the likes of me.

I remember while with the BBC, being asked to do commercials for a variety of firms that would, of course, be shown on ITV. One was for Ford tractors; another for an agro-chemical company and yet another was to advertise eggs for the Egg Marketing Board. There were others too that I forget, and I wasn't enthusiastic to cheapen myself with such vulgar things as commercials. But when the egg opportunity turned up I thought it was harmless enough and might help some of my fellow farmers to market their produce.

So, I asked one of my bosses at the Corporation if it would be OK to accept the Egg Boards invitation. This mild-mannered man suddenly became very aggressive indeed. "If you want to ruin your reputation and risk never working for the BBC again – go ahead", he said heatedly. "But I promise you I won't ever employ you again".

You have to remember that they were different times. There were only two TV channels – BBC and ITV. None of the others had been launched, and the prospect of hundreds of channels like we have today, wasn't even dreamed of as a possibility. Under such circumstances "artist exclusivity" really meant something. If you were seen on one channel, you were not welcome on the other. And as for getting involved with advertising – well, it was just not done if you valued your position. Needless to say, I turned down all subsequent requests to do commercials although the generous rewards offered had been tempting.

Even so, after a few years of run-of-the-mill earnings from my niche programmes and articles, I actually had a little money in the bank. Ever since getting the tenancy of Whiterails Farm I had worked as hard as possible, either on the farm, or earning money from other things, and I began to think I had earned a holiday. More particularly, Lorna, who by this time had had three children as well as looking after me, had more than earned a break.

My mind turned to those mountains I had seen and loved on school trips many years before, and to the possibility of having a go at skiing. We had a number of friends who already headed for the snow covered slopes for a week or two each winter, and I began to think of joining them.

One of my closest friends was Alan Alston, who sadly died early in 2021, had been on a few ski trips. Indeed he met his wife, Anne, on one to Obergurgl. I first met Alan when we were teenagers travelling on the same bus to school in Norwich. We didn't go to the same school, but they were close to one another and his bus route from his father's farm at Wymondham took him through Hethersett where I got on. We established a nodding acquaintanceship in the knowledge that we were both farmer's sons. But we didn't get close until Young Farmers. Then he went off to Korea to do his National Service after which he spent a year at Cirencester Agricultural College (I was exempted because I was milking cows, which was regarded as a key job) so we didn't meet for three years.

When he returned and re-joined Wymondham Young Farmers we found we hit it off really well, and started a tradition that continued until he passed away – having lunch together every Saturday. When I got married to Lorna I asked him to be my Best Man, which sealed our friendship even further. And when he met and married Anne, she and Lorna enjoyed one another's company as much as we did. It was a superb relationship that survived and deepened over the years.

In any event, when I mentioned skiing to Alan one Saturday lunchtime he thought it would be a good idea to make up a party to go to Switzerland. A few phone calls later and we had put together about a dozen like-minded people, some first timers, like myself, and some who had been skiing a few times. They included our nearest farming neighbours, Alan and Kate Barnard, Gavin Paterson, well known Friesian breeder and my predecessor as Chairman of Norfolk YFC, Jimmy Laurie, and of, course, Alan and Anne Alston. For the record Alan was Norfolk YFC Chairman the year after me, so it was very much an old Young Farmers party. We booked through Thomas Cook to go to Wengen in the Bernese Oberland of Switzerland, arranged for someone to come and live in our house and look after our children, and a few months later found ourselves at the Falken Hotel.

It was a cold sunny January, and the nursery slopes, just below the hotel, were continuously icy. Lorna and I went out each morning to join a ski class and attempted to make our long wooden ski's grip the icy slope. Suffice to say we fell a lot and bruised our backsides. And for the first few days I wondered if we had made the wrong decision by coming here. But whenever we looked up we saw graceful looking creatures in skin-tight ski trousers gliding past and making it look so easy. There's nothing like that to increase determination. And after a few days we began to get the hang of it. We didn't look graceful, but we began to be able to control our ski's.

At 30 plus we were, of course, starting too late. Really good skiers start when they are in short trousers and learn it like a language. But by the end of the fortnight we were boarding the train at Wengen station, which took us up under the shadow of the famous Eiger with the majestic Jungfrau in the middle distance, then sliding down to the bottom of one of the many T-bar lifts to pull us up to the start of another run, and so on. We would never emulate Jean Claude Killy, but it was starting to be enjoyable.

In the evenings we went to one of the many bars in town and watched mountain entertainment including yodelling put on by the locals or listened and danced to a trio in the hotel lounge. The pianist had a voice like a white Louis Armstrong, and yes, often sang What a Wonderful World. One evening we went curling under flood lights on the rink in the village. Another time we watched the locals ski-jumping. One day as I walked down the main street of Wengen, I recognised, coming the other way, one of my hero's, David Cornwell, aka John Le Carre, the author of spy thrillers, like Smileys People. He apparently lived in the village.

The following winter the same group of friends, plus a few more, went to Arosa. We arrived on the funicular railway in a massive snowstorm. In fact we had been delayed on the way up from the valley by a snow clearance train that had gone ahead to allow us to complete our journey. When we got off the train we traced our way along very narrow streets behind the sledge pulling our cases to our hotel. We only realised a few days later when workmen arrived with shovels that the streets were three times as wide but snow had buried cars parked either side of them to a depth of about six feet. We, indeed, had been on the last train into the resort for about three days – the time it took to clear the line.

But the skiing was so much more comfortable than Wengen's ice. Or rather, when you fell it was. And once the piste's had been levelled, they provided some of the best skiing I have ever enjoyed. Arosa was a very special and quite expensive village and had one of the best tea houses in the Alps. Although, when we all met up after skiing each day, hot chocolate was usually the drink of choice accompanied by a nutty tart.

You should be aware that Harold Wilson was Prime Minister of Britain at the time. The economy of the country was in all sorts of trouble, and to try to keep as much sterling in the country as possible the government had imposed a limit of £50 per person to be taken out of the country for holiday purposes. Frankly, that was not enough to pay for ski passes and a few nights out so we had to think out of the box. If you were on a business trip the regulations said you were allowed up to £200per day. So I used some of my journalistic contacts to organise business visits in association with our ski trips. The men in the party would leave the ladies in the nearest Swiss town to enjoy some shopping while we went off "on business".

I got us into the CIBA-GIEGY chemical factory near Basel; the Deutz combine factory near Rheinfall, an agricultural educational establishment near Berne; and best of all, a trip down the Simmental valley to look at a breed of cattle that some UK farmers had expressed a wish to import. The only imported breed to that point was the Charolais from France, and it had begun to make its mark. Would the Simmental be next?

We certainly liked what we saw down that valley and picked up a lot of information about the breed. And when I got back I wrote a column for the *Financial Times* advocating that the cattle should be allowed into the UK because of their dual purpose as both milk and meat animals; their good feet and versatility to withstand winters tied by the neck in sheds, and then climb the mountains to graze all summer. A few weeks after that article appeared the UK government granted permission to import Simmentals. I never did find out if my article had influenced the decision.

But our main immediate concern as we travelled back from the valley to collect our wives before heading for the slopes was the £200per day we had been permitted to take with us for our business trip. Arosa was one of the places our "business" had allowed us to go.

While there I lost a filling from one of my teeth. I didn't want to put up with a hole in my mouth for another week so arranged to visit a dentist in the village. "Ah, yes", he said, "I can see ze problem". I can fix it in a few minutes. But you are English. How are you going to pay me? You have a problem with your Mr Vilson, yes?" I said that yes, Mr Wilson was a problem, and I hoped he would remember that when he calculated the bill. He promised he would and with a broad smile mended my filling.

Altogether Lorna and I enjoyed about thirty skiing holidays with a varying group of friends, venturing into the Rockies in America as well as many places across Europe. When they were old enough we took our growing family and introduced them to the joys of snow. The skiing was great and so was the company, comprising as it always did farmers like ourselves. We had erudite conversations at times in the strangest of places.

One of our number, Jimmy Laurie, sadly no longer with us, was trying to design what was almost certainly the first ever slurry separator. For the uninitiated, cow dung has within it a high percentage of water. Storing it safely so as not to create pollution is one of the most expensive aspects of dairy farming. But he reasoned that if he could somehow squeeze most of the liquid out of it so that it could be pumped through an irrigation system it would be much easier to deal with. Furthermore that the solids would make good compost, and it too would be easier to handle and spread on the land.

I've lost count of the mountain restaurants in which we discussed the finer points of Jimmy's designs. But he did make a prototype machine to do what was intended and sold the patent to a manufacturer. The Idea has been copied and varied many times since and is now established as a concept all over the world where cows are kept. I've often wondered how much we should have claimed as design consultants for that winning idea.

One winter, when farming was having a relatively good year, and the Sterling/Swiss currency exchange rate was briefly in our favour, we even went to St Moritz. Full of "beautiful people" it was easy to see its appeal to those with pots of money. But the skiing was good too, and you never knew who you would run into on the slopes. I shared a ski lift with Jackie Stewart, the racing driver on one occasion.

And some of us decided to try the Cresta run, the course for which was in the town. That's the one where two- and four-men teams in sledges shaped like bullets, slide down a narrow gulley carved through the ice at ridiculous speeds. The deal was that you paid to ride between a professional "driver", although his influence on where the bobsled went in the gulley seemed severely limited by the speed at which it travelled, and a brake man behind who pushed the bobsled off at the top of the run, and then threw himself into the back of the contraption just before it reached full speed.

We were given a short talk on what we had to do on the ride, fitted with helmets, and then loaded up behind the driver. I don't suppose we went anything like as fast as competing teams, but I shall never forget the next one-minute-and-twenty-one-seconds. The G-forces as we speeded up and went round the corners, with the bob at a 90degree angle, to vertical were intense. We were told later they were almost equivalent to the forces experienced by astronauts on take-off. Whether that was true or not I cannot say but we certainly felt them, and I was rather pleased to feel the brake being applied when we approached the bottom of the run.

Shaking, we were helped out of the bobsled and transported back to the start in a four wheel drive and deposited back at the office where we were offered a double brandy to calm our nerves, then given a certificate to say we had done it signed by Gunther Sachs, the former husband of Bridget Bardot and President of the Club that owned the run.

Across the road from the Cresta there was another ice gulley in which you could, should you wish, do a solo run on a tiny sledge not much bigger than a tea tray. We watched a few brave souls having a go but decided we would leave the tea trays to others, and repaired to a café for another brandy and hot chocolate.

It wasn't until our third ski holiday, by which time we had graduated from beginner's classes to venturing around the slopes without instructors, that my journalistic instincts began to kick in. Every so often as we skied around, and sometimes as we were walking in the village of our choice that year we smelled cows. Poking our noses into where these aroma's seemed to be coming from, we soon found handfuls of cows tied by the neck in cramped sheds chewing hay. I took it on myself to find out more, and discovered that the cattle belonged to hotels, and farmers grazed their animals on the mountains in summer and brought them down into the sheds for the winter. Many of the farmers were the same people who had been teaching us to ski. They fed and milked the cows before ski classes in the morning, and then again in the evening, while we tourists were relaxing after a hard day on the slopes.

It was obvious that the holiday trade formed a key part of the farming economy. We hadn't started using the word diversification in Britain but that's what they were doing. We wondered how much of their income came from farming and how much from skiing. We suspected that skiing was the most remunerative. So, if that was correct, would the next generation continue to keep cows and farm or would they just concentrate on tourism?

But when we spoke to the owners of the cattle, some of whom had a few sheep as well, we learned that grazing animals were vital to the skiing economy. For if mountain grass was allowed to grow tall, when the snow came it would flatten it down the slope and the snow would run off. The grazing animals ate the grass down to a stubble which held the snow in place through the winter. Moreover, in alpine countries, governments give generous grants to maintain livestock on the hills for that purpose. In a way the idea is similar to our Less Favoured rea legislation, only much more generous.

We learned variations on this story in almost every European ski resort we visited and I took to writing columns about the phenomenon whenever we went skiing. Why didn't I just relax and enjoy myself instead of searching out stories to write about? My answer is that I enjoy finding out about such things and sharing the information with others in the hope that they find them interesting too. I do the same when I take parties to look at farming in other countries. I don't find it burdensome. It's fun. And I hope others enjoy reading about what goes on in other countries.

Chapter 21

Gap years for all the family

As each of our children completed their formal education we urged them to travel. I've heard it described as pushing them out of the nest to force them to fly on their own. I was only able to be pushed to a farm three miles away when I was their age, for reasons already discussed, but I had seen what foreign travel could do for countless other young people and was determined our lot should benefit from it too.

Andrew, our eldest, spent a couple of years at Brooksby Agricultural College in Leicestershire after school under the inspirational Principal, Ted Stearn. I had come across him in Norfolk years earlier and come to respect his teaching and his way with young people. That said he had his problems. He had been blown up during the 2nd World War and had lost an eye and a hand. So, he had an obvious glass eye and a tin hand over which he wore a leather glove – the kinds of disabilities young people might take advantage of. But he was so matter of fact about them and refused to allow them to cramp his style that everyone, young and old admired him.

When Andrew finished at Brooksby I told him he should travel for at least six months, and preferably a year, to learn how to earn a living and stand on his own feet. I told him I would buy him a return ticket to wherever he wanted to go and would provide £100 to get him started, as I would later do with each child in turn. After that they would be on their own. And I asked Andrew where he wanted to go?

He chose America and asked if I could contact some people I knew who were farming under pivot irrigators in Colorado and Texas to see if they had any jobs. I made the call and established there were possibilities and waved goodbye as he flew off to Dallas. From there he went to a small "one horse" town called Dalhart in the Texas panhandle, close to New Mexico, met up with the bosses of Western Ag Inc who offered him a job, and within weeks he was supervising the cropping under fifty or so centre pivot irrigators.

Here in Britain at the time we had never heard of centre pivot irrigation technology which was based on the fact that most of Mid-West America was divided into square Quarter Sections – that is a quarter of a square mile, or 160 acres. The centre of the irrigator was positioned in the middle of each block where a bore was sunk down to the available water, in this case from the Ogallala Aquifer. Water was pumped up the central pipe about eight feet high on top of which was a right-angled bend and a pivot. A ratchet mechanism on each wheeled tower supporting the quarter mile long irrigation boom, powered by the flow of water, drove the boom of the irrigator which reached the straight edges of the Section. Mounted on wheels the boom travelled 360 degrees around the central pivot so that water was sprinkled in a circle onto any crop growing under it. The corners were not irrigated but the land was relatively cheap so they were left fallow. Later models incorporated corner extensions that swung out automatically on corners and watered almost all of the land on the Quarter Section.

Needless to say this was exciting technology for a young man to be involved with, and very soon he was also helping to construct more of these irrigation systems as investors provided funds for the project to expand. We spoke on the phone across the Atlantic about once a week and one evening Andrew said "I'm not sure I'm coming home at the end of my six months here. The company has offered me a full-time job and I might be asked to go to Nebraska and then Saudi Arabia to erect irrigators there. Would that be OK with you?" I replied that so long as he was enjoying what he was doing he could stay as long as he liked. And so began an international career that was to take him around the world.

When our second son, Rob finished college – he too went to Brooksby – it was his turn to choose where to go. He'd made contact with some people who ran a horse stud in New South Wales, Australia and horses were always his hobby. He was also becoming interested in sheep. So it wasn't long before he set off for Sydney. He worked with stallions at the stud, then moved on to drive a huge tractor across fields bigger than he'd ever dreamed of, before finally getting his dream job of mustering sheep on horseback. Taking time off for a bit of a holiday and to spend some of the money he'd earned, he met up with a friend who was also "doing" Australia and they swam and sunbathed on an Island off Brisbane for a few days. Rob lost several layers of skin and got sunstroke. But there was no lasting damage.

Meanwhile, in the interests of sexual equality, Fiona needed a gap year. After she finished school at Hethersett Hall, very close to home, we persuaded her to attend the Norwich Technical College to do a secretarial course. She learned shorthand and typing but never really settled to the course. To try to promote more excitement in learning we arranged for her to have a year at a higher-class secretarial and "finishing" establishment in London. Again, she added to her knowledge but without much enthusiasm. We were realising by then that, like both her parents, she was, and remains essentially a country girl who enjoys rural pursuits.

In any event when it was her turn to go abroad I asked her where she fancied going? Her time at college hadn't all been wasted because she had learned about round the world flight tickets. "What I'd really like," she said, "is to fly to New Zealand, stay there for a while, then continue round the world, stopping off in America to see Andrew (who was by this time established over there) and then fly home".

I had given her the choice so had to honour what she wanted. And that's what she did, working her passage, like the boys, as she went. She found jobs in café's and on farms, and in orchards picking such things as kiwi fruit, before heading off over the Pacific to the USA. She stayed for a while with Andrew, experiencing her first earthquake, in Southern California and eventually arrived back in London.

She used her secretarial knowledge for a while before deciding she really wanted to train to be a florist at which she became very skilled. Indeed she still undertakes freelance commissions between looking after her husband, Stuart and their two sons, Angus and Monty, fulfilling her real vocation as a mother.

I hope and believe these experiences stood our family in good stead for later life. And I have recommended similar independence creating policies to lots of parents. Most of them have taken that advice. And the world has become a much smaller place these days. Smart phones, email, Skype and now Zoom and Teams are a doddle and very economical. Such technologies make distances seem much smaller, and you hardly feel separated by thousands of miles.

But back in the early 1980's we had to rely on the telephone. Direct dialling was just becoming possible but calls were expensive and you didn't want to chatter for long. But there was one call from America in 1982 which went on longer than most. Andrew called to say he had met a girl and that they planned to get married. She was called Rose Danda and she was a farmer's daughter from North Dakota.

The date for the wedding was subsequently set for July that year.

Dresses were bought, airline tickets were reserved and about thirty of our Norfolk friends decided to join us for the ceremony in The City of Michigan, North Dakota, population 296. This was real small-town America.

Sadly, however, before all this took place, my father became unwell. He went into hospital for an exploratory operation, during which it was discovered he had inoperable bowel cancer. His condition deteriorated fast and we began to wonder if we should postpone the American wedding. In the event he died about a week before the event and we went ahead with arrangements as they stood. But the occasion was obviously tinged with sadness. Father was 76 when he died.

After mother had passed away a few years previously father had renewed some of the activities he had had to put on hold during mother's illness – like singing and entertaining in halls all over Norfolk. It was great therapy for him, and helped lessen his loneliness. Indeed it seemed to us, his close family, that he was doing more concert party gigs than were good for him at his age. It soon became clear, however, that his incentive was not just to bathe in audience applause but also a comedienne called Brenda who often appeared on the same stages with him telling Norfolk stories.

Brenda was a schoolteacher and also a Methodist Local preacher, like father, and they quickly became very close. Before long another wedding was being planned and the family rejoiced that father had found someone with whom to share his old age. Sadly their time together was cut short by his cancer.

He was a good father and unlike some farmers who are reluctant to pass on responsibility to their families as they get older, he encouraged my brother and me all he could, and although not a demonstrative man, took obvious pride in what we both achieved. We miss him dreadfully.

Chapter 22

Show business

Back in my Young Farmer days I was invited to become a junior cattle steward at the Royal Norfolk Show, still held on the last Wednesday and Thursday in June each year, and occasionally slipping into July when the calendar dictates. This involved helping to co-ordinate the cattle judging in one of the rings; making sure the stockmen knew when their animals were due to be on parade; handing out rosettes to the prize winners; and generally ensuring the judge, invited by the Show Association, had everything he or she needed to do their job. I assisted the senior steward in charge of the Aberdeen Angus classes and thoroughly enjoyed the experience.

When all the cattle were judged and the rosettes fixed to their halters, we also had to take our judge to lunch in the judges and stewards' marquee, where all the other judges and stewards congregated for their midday meal. Top breeders of cattle, sheep, and pigs from around the country met, and still meet, in that marquee, and as a very junior steward I could hardly believe I was lunching next to nationally and sometimes internationally famous livestock farmers. It was a real privilege for a young lad like me, and I met and got to know some wonderful talented people.

But when I became involved in broadcasting and reporting on and from the Show for the BBC, I had to resign. I could not do both stewarding and reporting because my duties clashed, so reluctantly gave up stewarding. After a while, the BBC decided they did not want to cover regional agricultural shows, and I reverted for a few years to being just a regular visitor who derived enormous pleasure from attending the Show.

Then, one day, the Hon. Director of the Show, John Stimpson, phoned to ask if he could come and see me. John was a farmer with whom I had had some dealings because he was also chairman of the vining pea group of which we were a part. But he was also meticulous in his organisation of the Show and his dealings with its 300 or so volunteer stewards. This attention to detail may well have been drummed into him during the 2nd World War during which he had been ADC to General

Bernard Montgomery, or Monty, as he became known.

"I want to put a proposition to you", he said. "You will know that the long-standing Press Steward at the Show is getting rather old and he wants to retire. If you are willing I would like you to replace him". And he went on to tell me that he felt a more positive job could be done than had been in the past to encourage members of the press to feature the Show in their publications more often. He recognised that I was a member of the press fraternity as well as being a farmer and loyal Show attender and hoped that would enable me to achieve what he wished. He also discussed the delicacy of his request in that usually such tasks are allocated to those who had served in a junior capacity to whoever was retiring, whereas I had not been a steward for some years and was now being asked to leapfrog them and jump immediately to be a section Head Steward. He hoped my record in the media would be sufficient to deflect any criticism.

Obviously, I was flattered and accepted there and then. I said I would hope to improve relationships with my colleagues in the press throughout the year and not just on Show days. He allowed me to choose my junior stewards and we set about establishing year-round relationships with the media. I knew from experience that press people are pressurised to produce stories in short order, and that they were more likely to publish if they are provided with the facts in easily digested form. So, we started producing press releases that were not filled with dry statistics but told stories we hoped journalists would want to use. We also went out of our way to bring stories to them on press days and make their lives as easy as possible. Comments over the next few years appeared to indicate we had got it about right. One journalist said that previously he had felt those in charge had acted like policemen trying to make sure he and his fellow writers knew as little as possible of what was going on at the Show. Sadly, some farmers back then regarded journalists as enemies wanting to pry into their business. Perhaps we did a little, locally, to turn that situation around.

A few years later a stewarding vacancy arose in what was called the Education section of the Show and I was asked to add it to my "portfolio". Previously "Education" at the show had been interpreted as educating farmers to farm better. The annual exhibit under that heading had usually consisted of a few flat boards containing specific information about fertilisers or crop varieties with graphs and tables unintelligible to the non-specialist. Such exhibits seldom attracted many people and in my view, at a time when the means of communicating information to farmers were multiplying, were a waste of space.

I accepted responsibility for Education, provided I was permitted to educate consumers rather than farmers. We changed the entire focus and designed a stand that would appeal to children and their parents and might teach them a bit about farming and food production.

We set up a small bakery and arranged continuous demonstrations of grinding wheat, kneading dough, and baking bread. The smell of baking brought in hundreds all day. We had a churn making butter, and visitors could watch as liquid milk became solid butter. Kids shaped it into pats, and parents looked on fondly and learned too.

We got some fertile eggs almost ready to hatch in a small incubator with a glass front, and during the Show chicks could be seen pecking their way out of the shells. The only trouble was that there was a continuous scrap for the best positions to see it happening.

We grew plots of barley and had a micro- brewery making beer. We planted a temporary hedge around the stand to illustrate its value in providing a habitat for birds and for conservation.

We set up simple quizzes for children with answers to the questions available on the stand then gave away a few simple prizes. And the Education stand became one of the most popular on the showground.

As a Head Steward I was ex-officio a member of the ruling Council and the Executive Committee. After a year or two I was asked to be chairman of the Executive Committee which essentially took all the executive decisions to run the Association. The business of the Association was becoming bigger year by year, and under the guidance of Sir Timothy Colman, the Chairman of Council, we held a strategy meeting to decide how to divide responsibility for the different activities.

The Association had been a charity for many years and as such was exempt from income tax. But we were letting the ground for an increasing number of other activities which earned money for the Association but could hardly be described as charitable. On legal advice we set up a limited company alongside the charity whose job was to conduct all the commercial letting business, and which would donate its profits to the charity. By this time the Association had an annual income of close to £1million and a balance sheet worth nearly £4million, and unlike some County shows was usually profitable.

Norfolk has claimed for years that it was the biggest two-day agricultural Show in the country. It has maintained that position, I would claim, by sticking to its agricultural and countryside roots. That is not to say it does not feature other things. There are lines of motor vehicles, there are stands that sell non-agricultural things for visitors to buy. But we have always given farm related exhibitors preferential rates for their stands, and we have always tried to be true to our rural history. Indeed the money earned from outside lettings goes towards funding the kind of Show we, its members, want to see.

The Council is very much aware that Norfolk saw some of the first agricultural shows in Britain. Holkham Sheep Shearings, hosted by Thomas William Coke on his estate in North Norfolk, were arguably, along with similar events hosted by the Duke of Bedford at Woburn, the forerunners of agricultural shows. It is a tradition Norfolk will not surrender lightly.

During my period as Executive Committee Chairman I had the enormous privilege of welcoming many distinguished Presidents, including the man who, at the time, occupied Holkham Hall, Lord Leicester, a direct descendant of Thomas William Coke. His son Tom has now taken up residence in the Hall with his young family. HM The Queen and Prince Philip honoured us with their presence as show Presidents, as did The Princess Royal, not to mention a couple of Ministers of Agriculture, John MacGregor and Gillian Shephard, both of whom had Norfolk constituencies before they were elevated to the House of Lords.

As previously stated I have always believed it wrong to stay on in a role too long. We all have ideas on how things should be done and while we can influence such things it is right to do so. But it is also right after, say, six to nine years, to move on and allow someone else the same privilege you have enjoyed. By that time you have probably run out of fresh ideas anyway. My chairmanship of the RNAA Executive Committee lasted ten years, so I am not entirely consistent. But I really felt I should step down after that slightly overlong period. Then, to my amazement and delight the Council asked me to be President. Never in my wildest dreams did I ever expect to be bracketed with those who had served as President before. But it was an honour I shall always cherish and one which Lorna was able to enjoy with me.

Having been involved with the RNAA for so many years in different roles I thought I knew most of what went on and would not be surprised by anything my Presidency revealed. How wrong I was. As President you are escorted to places on the showground you were only vaguely aware of previously. We went to see the Household Cavalry temporary barracks on the showground where they clean their tack and brush their horses. We talked to several of the soldiers some of whom turned out to be young women. We talked to many exhibitors about why they attend the show and whether they could measure the cost of it commercially. We walked the cattle lines with the Head Steward as guide and wondered at how far some exhibitors had come. Some told us The Royal Norfolk Show was the best cattle show in the country; somewhat of a surprise when you consider how few head of livestock we now have in the County.

But one of the biggest surprises was when my fellow stewards and old mates started doffing their bowlers at me and calling me Mr President without any obvious sign of irony. The office really does demand respect, it seems, whoever holds it and I was quite taken aback. That said those same mates who doffed their hats while I was President are back taking the mickey now I no longer carry that authority. So, it didn't last. But it was nice while it did.

Chapter 23

The Oxford Farming Conference

Agricultural Shows, some of which have lasted for between 150 and 200 years, were initiated by farmers and landowners to spread good farming practice and emerging knowledge. The Royal Show, sadly no longer with us, adopted the motto" Practice with Science", and that broad concept inspired county shows as well. Declining numbers of farmers willing to give up their time to help run them, urbanisation and in some cases poor financial management has reduced the number of shows across the country to a fraction of what there were. Those that have disappeared have left country life in the areas in which they used to operate much the poorer, and in my view contributed to the loneliness experienced by some of today's farmers.

Like weekly markets, which have also declined in number, they had a social as well as a business function, and when they are not there the opportunities to talk over problems with like-minded people are lost. This has become more serious as manpower on farms has been replaced by horsepower. I'm not saying mechanisation is wrong – indeed it is inevitable and has enabled farmers to survive and produce food for the nation at low cost. But when it leads, as it has in many cases, to a farmer working alone all day and every day, feeding stock, driving tractors, and in the evenings calculating wages and VAT, filling in forms, depression can set in and suicide can result. The Rural Stress Unit, based at Stoneleigh, has never been busier.

Another institution that grew out of adversity in the depressed 1930's was the Oxford Farming Conference. A group of farmers surrounding Oxford decided to hold an annual conference to discuss their problems and listen to speakers who might have some of the answers. At the time the University of Oxford ran agricultural courses, and the conference soon became centred on that seat of learning. It quickly earned a reputation as a forum for independent thought, and has continued, apart from the period of the 2nd World War, until now it is bigger and more prestigious than ever.

I first went to it as a radio reporter for *On Your Farm* with producer, Tony Parkin, in 1964. I interviewed academics, politicians and some farmers who had given papers at the event. I almost began to feel I was at the university I never attended. And when the opportunity came to do the same again the following year I jumped at the chance. Suffice to say I was hooked, not only by the quality of most of the speakers but also by the chance to mix and speak to and befriend the industry leaders who frequented the conference.

I attended fifty conferences without a break and was inspired by several of them. I remember coming home from one, for instance, fired up to expand our pig herd. I worked out a strategy, costed it and discussed it with my father, and within months had set in train a building and breeding programme that was to double our production of pigs. Oxford really is a place where you go to recharge your batteries.

At least it was when most of those attending were farmers and, by definition, most of those arranging it were also practicing farmers. Sadly, in my view, the costs of attending and paying for overnight accommodation for two or three nights has become too high for many farmers struggling to control outgoings. Attendance now seems to be dominated by land agents, rural solicitors, farm accountants, bank managers and consultants. Inevitably the organisers are chosen from such people so the imbalance is self-perpetuating. True the organisers provide bursaries for young farmers and that is a good thing. But it's not self-generating like it used to be. Perhaps I am exaggerating the problem because I remember the old days and am resisting change. Whatever! I have seldom felt as inspired by Oxford in recent years as I was in those early days. The other criticism I would make of modern Oxfords is that they feature far too many politicians who seldom add anything to existing knowledge and tend to use the event to promote their party's policies.

In any event, during the vintage years I was asked to give papers on three or four occasions, and sat as a member of discussion panels a couple of times as well. Then, in 1981 I was asked to join the organising committee – a three-year appointment. I agreed, but it was a difficult time to do so. Veteran Oxford Professor, Mike Soper, who had been organising secretary since the War, finally decided to retire aged about 80. He insisted that his successor must be another Oxford man and nominated a younger colleague who none of us knew.

It soon became clear that this candidate's heart wasn't in the job. Meetings were haphazard; minutes weren't kept; and we later discovered the finances were soon in a mess too. Not wanting to upset Mike Soper we decided to try to work with his nominee for another year. This was a mistake. By the end of that second year there were no audited accounts, no reserves, no proper records, and the conference was on its knees. It was at this point that the rest of the committee asked me to be their chairman, which implied chairing the committee and the conference the following year.

I accepted, but said I refused to work with the person who had let us down so badly; that we must find a new secretary as a matter of urgency. I also insisted that for the first time ever there should be a vice chairman. The man I chose was Poul Christiansen who had a dairy farm just outside Oxford. He later went on to become Chairman of Natural England and President of the National Federation of Young Farmers Clubs.

Between us we persuaded a man called Jimmy Elliott, who ran The Weed Research Institute at Kidlington, just east of Oxford, to take on the voluntary job. Jimmy had been a regular at Oxford conferences for many years and had a good idea of what was required. Indeed he would have been the person most of us would have chosen for the task a couple of years previously had it not been for Mike Soper's influence.

Suddenly things began to happen as they should. I remember sitting with Jimmy in his office at Kidlington planning future strategy, when we realised the Conference had no proper constitution; that the appointment of committee members, including us, had been completely informal. Further, that should there be a snowstorm the following January and no-one turned up we, the informal members of the committee would be jointly and severally liable for all the costs of rooms, dinners and so on for several hundred delegates. We also discovered there was no computerised delegate list; that invitations had historically been done longhand and were based on handwritten notes in a dog eared exercise book.

Clearly there was more to do than just organise a conference for the following January. Jimmy set about constructing a computerised delegate list, and we sought legal advice on setting up a limited liability company to limit our risk if it snowed. We had about £5 in the bank, so we also had to be careful not to bankrupt the conference.

The committee met a few times and we came up with some speakers we thought would be good, including my old friend Henry Plumb, who by this time had left the NFU presidency and become MEP for Gloucestershire. Letters were written inviting the chosen ones, and by late summer we seemed to be making progress on all fronts. Then, in August, Jimmy Elliott went for a sailing holiday on his boat in the Solent, had a heart attack while out on the water, and died.

It was a terrible tragedy for his family. But it was rather serious for the Oxford Conference committee too. We were faced with picking up the pieces Jimmy had left half done, completing the programme and the accommodation and meal arrangements in Oxford, and finding someone to be secretary for the next years committee.

I asked Poul Christiansen if he would deal with the beds and the meals in Oxford and he readily agreed. Meanwhile I undertook most of the rest. I estimate it took me two days a week from September to December to pull all the loose ends together. Much of that time was taken up finding a new secretary.

I enjoyed a close relationship with ICI at the time, partly because ours was an ICI costed farm – a valuable service the fertiliser company offered to its customers – and partly because of deals I was doing with them for Loddon Farmers members, the co-operative of which I was then chairman. I had heard on the grapevine that Ken Nelson, an affable Northern Irishman, might be running down his role running the costings scheme, and might be looking for part time employment. Enquiries revealed the rumours were true, but discussions with Ken showed he could not afford to work for nothing. So, I took it upon myself to negotiate with ICI to second Ken to the conference for a year or two with ICI paying him.

My ploy worked and I secured the secretariat for the immediate future. But some of the old guard who had been attending the conference since the 1930's were appalled that I had accepted money from a commercial company to help run the conference. "Its independence is sacrosanct", they said, and I was a persona non grata for a while. What those critics would think now of an event that is dominated by commercial sponsorship I don't know but I confess that the rot set in with me.

My committee never did finish setting up the computer register of delegates, nor did we complete the limited company arrangements. There were too many other things to do in a short time. But our committee member successors at least had a head start, and before long they were calling themselves company directors. These days, with all the sponsorship the conference attracts, the directors have sizeable reserves at the bank, and even treat themselves to dinner at the Farmers Club in London when they meet. In my year, the committee realised the conference was so short of cash that we even paid for our own tickets.

Chapter 24

Associated Farmers/Sentry

In 1983 the UK government launched a Business Expansion Scheme. It provided tax breaks for people with money to encourage them to invest in industry and thereby create more jobs. I registered the launch but took little notice of it as it did not seem to be relevant to farming. Then a land agent friend, Nick Reiss, who lived in our village, came to see me. He told how he and a bunch of Norwich based professionals; a solicitor, an accountant and an investment manager and himself, had been looking at the details of the scheme and concluded it could be applied to agriculture. He went on to ask if I would like to be involved.

I said I could not see how an investment in farmland would create many jobs at a time when farm labour forces were being reduced. He pointed out that it would create some jobs, and that in any case he and his colleagues needed a real farmer to join their group to give it credibility. I was a bit half-hearted about the project, but said if it meant the investors, whom it was assumed would mainly be city dwellers, would learn more about the reality of farming, I'd give it a go. I wouldn't call it high finance, but it was the nearest I had come to it at the time.

A prospectus was drawn up, a London agent was selected, and on the appointed day we travelled to the City to launch what we had called Associated Farmers. Sitting in the London agent's office I got my first sight of the printed prospectus. I had agreed the content with my Norwich colleagues, of course, but the agent had designed the cover. It featured a drawing of wide-open countryside with no animals, and hardly a tree or hedge in sight. It was just the kind of scene I had been so keen to eliminate from the countryside, and I was appalled. But it was too late to do anything about it and the launch went ahead.

I was equally appalled at the way the agent invited some colleagues and press to the event. An hour before it was due to start he sat at his desk in full view of my colleagues and myself and phoned a few numbers. "I say Julian" (or some other name), he said, "We've got a little launch on in a while. Would you like to pop along?" As it turned out he did manage to gather a handful of people to his office and they went off with the awful looking prospectus. And for that, in my view, most unprofessional service, he charged a fat fee that came, of course, from the investor's cash when it started to arrive. This, I began to realise, was how City people operated. I expressed my disgust to my colleagues, but there was not much else I could do – other than resign. I decided to stick with it in the determined hope that my original intentions might be realised if and when we bought a farm.

Despite the cover of the prospectus, we attracted a few hundred small investors whose money enabled us to buy a 600 acre farm near Ipswich in Suffolk, and I set about trying to influence its management. We employed the two men who were already working on the farm, and found a local young farmer who was keen to use the buildings to finish beef cattle. I invited Suffolk County Council's environmental advisor, Melinda Appleby, to visit and walk round the place and suggest how we could improve wildlife habitats on the place, and what to do with the area of ancient woodland we had acquired with the farmland.

Within a few months we had improved the hedges and planted trees in unproductive corners; invited a gang of Suffolk's unemployed, who, under supervision, coppiced the wood into rides which allowed sunlight to penetrate to the woodland floor and encouraged the growth of carpets of spring flowers such as bluebells; and made the young farmer, John Baker, our manager as well as our beef finishing partner. I was beginning to be able to live with my conscience. Indeed, we held our first AGM on the farm the following year and took the investors round on trailers. Gratifyingly some of them came up to me afterwards and said, "Thank you for the way you are looking after our farm".

1984 was a good year for cereals, and like many farmers Associated Farmers harvested the best yields to date. Things were going well for the investors, and a year or two later we were offered the tenancy of about 500 acres at Burnham Market in North Norfolk. It was good sugar beet and barley land, whereas the Suffolk farm was more suited to wheat and rape, and we jumped at the chance to expand our operation. John Baker, our established manager, moved to Burnham Market to take on the extra responsibility but continued to control the first farm. The Norfolk farm mill pond was home to great Crested Newts, and some of the arable land was a regular stopping off place for a migratory flock of Pink Footed Geese that enjoyed grazing our sugar beet tops each winter. Our shareholders were delighted and we were able to show them a profit.

A few years after that Nick Reiss, who was a partner with Brown & Co, discovered that the Coal Board Pension Fund who had purchased Norfolk's biggest farming company some years before had decided to dispose of it. Months of tortuous negotiations later he had persuaded City institution Equity & Life to buy most of the estate, which ran to about 9,000 acres, and for Associated Farmers to manage half of it.

Once again our trusted farm manager, John Baker, moved house – this time to Cantley, alongside Britain's first sugar beet factory. The farm had, in fact, been bought by Dutch financiers when they had funded the building of it in 1912, as a place where they could teach Norfolk farmers to grow sugar beet. This was a huge expansion for us and for John, for he continued to manage the other two farms from this new base. This time we inherited a poultry unit producing chickens for meat, and a herd of dairy cows which grazed the marshes that were an integral part of the farm, as well as a considerable acreage of good arable land. Again, the marshes pleased our investors as they were part of a complex of low-lying grassland just inland from Great Yarmouth that were well known as one of East Anglia's best conservation areas.

The most difficult part of taking over the farm was that it employed far too many men. Arthur Scargill, the mineworkers champion and Union Leader, had decreed that no workers should lose their jobs while his pension fund owned it. Consequently it had been loss making and this was almost certainly the reason it had been sold. All of which left us to tidy up the mess.

One by one we interviewed every member of staff. They weren't daft. They knew very well that there were too many of them for the farm to be profitable. We told those we were able to keep that they still had a job, and then had the unenviable task of telling about half of them that we had to make them redundant. It wasn't a day I enjoyed, and disposing of jobs was hardly in the spirit of why we had been initiated. But it had to be done. We gave generous redundancy packages, allowed those leaving to stay in their service houses for extended periods, and wrote lots of references. I'm pleased to say that within a couple of months all those made redundant, with the exception of one seventy-year-old lady calf feeder, had found other employment and some had the grace to come and tell us we had done them a favour.

But these were exciting times. Associated Farmers had been the vehicle that had enabled quite speedy expansion, and a growing business provides focus and satisfaction for all involved. Our financial advisors saw the possibility of further expansion, provided we could attract more investors, and suggested we should apply to join the Third Market of the London Stock Exchange, set up specifically for small businesses like ours. More meetings followed and more trips to London, and in due course we became a quoted company on the Stock Exchange – albeit a very small one. This meant there was a market for our shares and people could buy and sell them. Very soon our shareholder profile started to change from the original investors who wanted to get a tax benefit and own a slice of land, to speculators some of whom had different ambitions.

By now Associated Farmers had been in existence for about ten years. Then another opportunity to expand presented itself. Sentry Farming, from whom we had bought the original farm near Ipswich, approached us to see if we might be interested in a merger. Sentry had been going for longer than Associated Farmers, and was managing over 30,000 acres across the south and east of England. The Sentry people clearly had more experience and expertise than us, but we had a Stock Exchange quote and that was attractive to them.

Suffice to say both parties realised there were synergies between us and, once again after many more meetings, we decided to merge. Sentry was the longest established and the best known, so we adopted their name and Associated Farmers was closed. And I found myself part of a bigger farming company than I could ever have imagined as a boy starting out. I also soon took great pleasure in belonging to a company which employed and trained young men to be skilled farm managers, and which provided a farming ladder up which they could climb. Sentry's ethos already recognised the importance of conservation alongside production, and as a Director of the company I was able to encourage that to develop further. I also undertook to arrange and chair an annual conference for Sentry that developed and attracted 400 to 500 delegates.

The mid 1990's was not a happy time for me at Sentry. An influential investor had acquired a significant proportion of the shares and insisted we apply for full listing on the Stock Exchange. I did not think we were big enough and said so but it happened anyway. Sadly the costs of compliance with Stock Exchange rules was prohibitive and swallowed up most of Sentry's margins during a difficult time for farming. My opposition was not appreciated and I was voted off the board. The overambitious director disappeared and soon after that the executives of the company were forced to do a management buy-out. I was invited back as a Trustee of the new board structure, in which most of the shares are owned by employees.

Over the years I have watched as young trainees, still wet behind the ears, have developed into senior managers whose influence on Sentry and across the industry is immense and still growing. People say there is no chance for the young to get into farming these days except by inheritance or marriage. On the face of it, with land prices soaring into the stratosphere, and FBT rents following behind, or in some cases leading the way, it may be difficult to disagree. But in no other major industry is it expected that many of those working in it should become the boss. A farm management company, or a kind of management co-operative as Sentry is, provides a career structure for young people to acquire training, secure employment and promotion on merit. It can provide the much-loved experience of farming, dealing with the countryside, living in the middle of what you manage - and a guaranteed salary. Sadly that last item is not guaranteed to all who farm in their own right. The rewards and satisfaction of working for a good farm management company should not be underestimated.

Chapter 25

LEAF

Criticism of farming continued and increased during the 1980's as "food mountains, milk lakes, and wine lakes" appeared to grow. "Why are we paying farmers huge subsidies for producing what nobody wants" was the loud and repeated chorus. It meant the industry was on the back foot and attracted further criticism about the damage farming was doing to the countryside. I defended my farming colleagues as best I could but recognised there was some truth in what was being said. As always, however, the criticism often relied on half-truths and innuendo which created a perception among consumers and taxpayers that the situation was worse than in reality it was. This in turn persuaded the media that farming was a soft target which it could attack with impunity.

By this time I was spending two or three days a week with Anglia TV presenting *Farming Diary* and filming stories for it as well as making other countryside-based programmes about rural personalities under the title *Country People,* and anything else the company thought I could turn my hand to. But when it came to programmes attacking farming I was by-passed in favour of producers who came at the subject from a hyper-critical background.

One in particular was in the habit of greeting me in the staff canteen where we all lunched with comments like "Ah, here's the subsidy king. How many hedges have you ripped out this week and how many people have you poisoned?" It was, of course, his idea of a joke but I found it difficult to take it as amusing – although I tried to smile so as to let him and others who heard him know I wasn't taking him seriously.

That same producer was given the task of making a half hour film on how farmers were polluting the Norfolk Broads. I was excluded from the project but kept an eye on what he was doing through one or two friends in the company who were involved. Needless to say he took lots of footage of sprayers and fertiliser spreaders and intercut them with shots of water covered in green algae. He couldn't find enough algae on the water of the Broads, so filmed static ponds in close-up and implied that they were part of the area where holiday makers had to swim and sail.

He also wanted to illustrate how he thought farmers caused water pollution and the effect this had on wildfowl living on the Broads. He had heard of a few cases of botulism among ducks that had supposedly consumed bacteria from the water and searched the Broads to find some that had died of it to include in his film. Having failed he went to a Norwich butchers selling game birds in feather; bought half a dozen of them; laid them at the edge of one of the Broads; smeared them with mud and took his pictures.

I cannot swear that farm pollution has never caused botulism that has killed ducks. But I can vouch for the fact that water and sewage companies have admitted they caused pollution in the past because of leaky pipes and inadequate purification. And it used to be the case that pollution was caused by leisure craft holidaying on the Broads. The practice of emptying sewage into the water from such boats has long been banned. But it wasn't just farmers that were guilty of pollution, and the kind of misrepresentation this TV producer perpetrated was not untypical of what farmers were up against from all sectors of the media through the decade of the 1980's.

I came to the conclusion that the industry must fight back to stem this damaging tide. On the farm we had been active members of FWAG (Farming And Wildlife Group) for some years, and were following their recommendations on hedgerow management. But this was only really dealing with field boundaries and ponds, and I was sure we needed something that dealt with what we did in the middle of the field – in other words where we grew crops. I was in the fortunate position of meeting industry leaders on a regular basis as I interviewed them for the programmes with which I was involved. I challenged such people regularly to do more; to find scientists and others to refute the most serious allegations; to improve their organisations' public relations. The answer always came back that they were doing all that was possible and affordable. But it clearly wasn't enough.

I issued the same kinds of challenges to captains of allied industries – the companies that, in many cases, were supplying the products to farmers which were attracting most of the criticism. Why, I asked them, did they not co-operate with one another to deal with the critics? How about a fund to which they could all contribute to help turn unscientific arguments back onto the critics? Almost to a man the industry bosses replied that they could not possibly co-operate with their competitors;

that they had their own PR departments and they were doing the best they could.

Throughout this time I was writing weekly columns for the magazine *Big Farm Weekly* and would often make the same sort of arguments stressing that we, the farmers, needed to raise our game when it came to caring for the countryside and that this would help negate some of the critic's allegations.

It was, I believe, these articles that attracted the attention of some conference organisers in the USA. In the autumn of 1990 they invited me to speak at an event in Memphis, Tennessee where the theme was to be improving farming sustainability. I accepted and took as my theme the fact that sustainability has many meanings and I mentioned a few of them. There is sustainability of yield which is vital for a successful business; sustainability of the countryside which implies maintaining habitats and biodiversity to ensure the survival of species and a few others. But arguably the most important definition of sustainability is profit, because without profit none of the others are possible. I therefore advocated that any attempt to improve the sustainability of agriculture must start with profitability.

My message seemed to go down well with most of the US audience although there were a few non farmers present who, predictably, felt profit was a dirty word. On the flight home I sat next to a senior person from Zeneca who had attended the same conference. "I liked what you said", he told me, "What are you going to do about it?"

We had a six-hour flight ahead of us, so I told him what I had been trying to do already, and of the negative responses I had had from people like him. I said that given the chance, and some funding, I would set up an initiative to improve the image of farming. But it must be more than a thin veneer of PR, I went on, it must really mean something, and farmers who got involved must believe in what they were doing and be prepared to open their farms and show what they do to the world.

My flying friend sat quietly through my diatribe and when I had finished he asked whether I was aware that an initiative similar to what I had described was about to be set up in Germany and would be funded by ECPA, the European Crop Protection Association, consisting of the twelve agrochemical manufacturers then operating across Europe. "It's going to be called Integrated Crop Management" he concluded.

"Who on earth is going to know what that is?" I retorted, "They need to change the name to start with". "Be that as it may", he went on, "if I could persuade ECPA to come up with some funding to start something in the UK, would you be prepared to be involved?" I said that yes, I would, but that it would have to be called something more friendly. And there and then over the mid-Atlantic we thought up *Linking Environment And Farming*, and I drew the obvious logo with the acronym LEAF inside it on the back of an airline menu.

True to his word, my friend went to work on ECPA, and they promised £70,000 per year for three years. Meetings were held in London, at the 2nd of which I was made chairman, and in 1991 LEAF the charity was born. But at that stage it was just an idea that needed fleshing out. We also needed people to run it and an office for a base.

George Jackson was the Director of the Royal Agricultural Society of England (RASE) at Stoneleigh Park, Warwickshire, then the home of the Royal Show and he was very supportive of the whole concept. He found us a small office and agreed to join me in selecting someone to run it. We advertised for a co-ordinator and had several replies. We shortlisted the applicants down to six and the day of the interviews arrived. That morning one of the six cried off because he had been offered another job. So, we were left with five candidates. George and I interviewed the first four and agreed that none of them were suitable. We were feeling a bit depressed.

Then in walked a young lady called Caroline Drummond. She was working as a warden and lecturer at Shuttleworth Agricultural College in Bedfordshire and told us the job we had advertised read like her dream job. An hour later George and I were both feeling much happier. We were pretty sure she was the one we were looking for. But we didn't quite trust our judgement given how desperate we had felt about the others, so we arranged to travel to Bedfordshire the following week and treated Caroline to supper in a pub near the College. Two hours later we were sure and offered Caroline the job. And the rest, as they say is history.

We launched LEAF at the Royal Show in July 1991, by which time Caroline had recruited Justine Hards as her assistant. And the LEAF admin team consisted of two Little Women. But they packed a punch. We organised a structure of committees consisting of like-minded people from a range of interest groups across the industry and we were in business. At first, committee members from the NFU and the CLA

170

did not know whether to trust us and more particularly members from the RSPB and the CPRE who we had included in our structure. But over a couple of years of straight dealing (yes it took that long) we managed to build up a mutual trust between these organisation and LEAF which gradually spread so that they began to trust one another. We had created a dialogue of stake holders which survives to this day, and has been crucial to the growing influence of LEAF and its achievements.

One of LEAF's greatest accomplishments was that DEFRA adopted a version of Integrated Farm Management (which since I had rejected its close relation, Integrated Crop Management had come into common parlance) as its received and approved policy for British Agriculture. The NFU too has come in behind what LEAF has done, and although in our early days they treated us with some suspicion, today they advocate IFM. Most of Britain's top supermarkets now insist that the fresh produce they sell must be grown to LEAF standards (although it is disappointing that not all of them advertise the fact). That farmers have completed the LEAF Environmental Audit has become a requirement for many buyers of a variety of produce, and growers of Oil Seed Rape can achieve a premium price provided they comply with the standards.

In fact it is now calculated that at least 45% of all the fruit and veg consumed in the UK is produced to LEAF Marque standards. It operates in 21 countries and has about 50 demonstration farms in the UK. My 1991 vision of a LEAF logo on every farm gate matched by the same image on every product on supermarket shelves has not quite been realised but it's getting closer all the time.

LEAF organises *Open Farm Sunday* during which several hundred thousand people take advantage of this annual event to visit a farm. It has added up over the years into the millions, over 90% of whom said they had learned more about food and farming from their visit. During the Covid19 lock-down these were replaced by virtual on-line visits, and once again hundreds of thousands joined from their sitting rooms.

And there is a network of more than a dozen demonstration farms and innovation centres, essentially research and education establishments, across the country where farmers can go to learn more about sustainability and environmental care. There are many other initiatives run from the modest office still on the Royal Showground even though the Show is no more.

Most gratifying has been the role that LEAF has played in showing how it is possible to optimise yield and profit while at the same time ensuring that the environment in which it takes place can be enhanced and made more friendly to wildlife. Some of the more extreme conservation bodies still insist it has to be one or the other; that you cannot do what is necessary to feed the world and look after the countryside and the creatures that live in it at the same time. On our farm we have always tried to do both, and LEAF has made that credible to all who approach the subject with an open mind.

I chaired and helped to guide LEAF for the first ten years of its existence and then, while remaining an ardent supporter, stood back and invited others with new and more modern ideas to take it forward. I have been proud and thrilled at what has been achieved. The team that has grown since my day has exceeded my expectations. Helping to start LEAF was one of the best and most satisfying things I have done in my life, and appointing Caroline Drummond (along with George Jackson) turned out to be an inspired choice. She is a high achiever and a great leader on behalf of the farming industry as the honours and positions she holds clearly illustrate. I thank and congratulate her on what she has done.

Chapter 26

The London Farmers Club

In 1965 as my broadcasting activities began taking me to London on a fairly regular basis – the BBC at Portland Place, just along from Oxford Circus was the HQ of the Corporation's national farming team and I often "borrowed" a studio there to record interviews for *On Your Farm* – I was persuaded by my producer, Tony Parkin, to join the London Farmers Club. For those who have never been there, it is in Whitehall Court just a stone's throw from Whitehall Place, which was the home of the Ministry of Agriculture until Labour Minister Jack Cunningham decided that was not grand enough for him, and moved the offices to Smith Square where DEFRA still resides today.

You look for a blue porch on which is a big number 3 and that's it. In the lobby there's a desk, usually manned by a couple of security men. For this is not only the entrance to the Club, it is also the way in to numerous private flats that occupy the same block. The Club itself is on the 1st floor, or the "Upper Ground" floor as the sign in the lift quaintly puts it. But there is also a flight of stairs beside the security desk and most farmers use them rather than wait for the lift which may be carrying residents to or from any of the seven floors above.

Having arrived at the "Upper Ground" the first thing you see is the Club's reception desk behind which sit a couple of helpful young ladies. At least that is what you find now. Until late 2014 one of the chairs was normally occupied by a small Irishman called Cyril who, until his retirement had been part of the fixtures and fittings for years. And if you don't see someone you know in the reception area (which you probably will) continue to the right towards the lounge area and the bar, and you almost certainly will meet someone you either know or recognise as being a well-known figure in the farming industry.

Over the years I have stayed in many hotels and eaten in many restaurants around the world. When you're travelling alone and don't know anybody it can be lonely and boring. But that is not the case at The Farmers Club. Even if you don't know anyone when you get there you will start a conversation with another farmer within minutes of going into the bar and suddenly you've made a new friend.

The restaurant has what is called the "Club" table which any member can join at breakfast or dinner rather than eating alone. And you might find yourself sitting next to a rural bishop, a member of the House of Lords, a dairy farmer from Cheshire, a potato grower from Scotland, a small holder from the fens, a vet who sits on a government committee, or whoever happens to be there that day.

Whenever I'm in London and need a meal or a bed I head for the Club. The food is all sourced from UK farmers, as you would expect, and the service is by charming chaps and ladies, some of whom have been there for many years, who call their regulars by name. Indeed the staff are like friends to members and they genuinely seem pleased to serve you. It is a club in every sense of the word and there isn't a better place for a farmer or someone in an ancillary trade, to stay in London.

The trouble is this has become so widely known by the members that it is sometimes difficult to get a room. The Club has over fifty bedrooms and during the week, from Monday to Thursday they fill up very quickly. Weekends are easier but few business meetings are held on Saturdays and Sundays, which is why many members use the Club. It's mainly families or theatre goers who use the facilities at weekends and reservations are relatively easy to get. If I think I might need a bedroom during the week I tend to try to book it some weeks ahead. Then if arrangements change there is a no charge cancellation policy provided it's done a couple of days before.

A few years ago the property next door, between the Club and the Ministry of Defence, came on the market. Had the Club been able to buy it most of the booking problems could, in theory, have been solved. Several new bedrooms could have been created and more and bigger public rooms as well. The Club appointed a sub-committee to try to buy the property but in the end the price it sold for was well above the value put on it by expert advisers to the Club and would have been a drain on resources for years had the Club tried to match it. So, sadly the problem of over popularity goes on despite some imaginative reorganisation of what was there before which has marginally increased the accommodation.

For most of my membership I have used the Club for meetings, meals, and accommodation like any other ordinary member. I remember being in London for a couple of meetings in the autumn of 1991. I had been to a conference at the Queen Elizabeth Centre in Westminster in the morning and had an appointment at the South African High Commission in Trafalgar Square in the afternoon. I was planning a study tour to South Africa the following spring and I wanted to speak to the Agricultural Attaché to see if he could give me any leads and information.

I walked along Whitehall, past the Cenotaph, to the Club and ordered a beer and a sandwich for a snack lunch from Rosemary, the barmaid who, like Cyril was Irish, and had been there even longer than him. She too has retired but she had the happy knack of remembering every member's name even if they hadn't been in the Club for a while, and in most cases what they usually drank. I had just ordered my sandwich when two men walked in and up to the bar beside me. Before I could greet them one of them stuck out his hand and said "Hello, I'm from South Africa. Are you a farmer?"

I replied that yes, I was, and welcomed him to the Club. He continued in that clipped accent all South Africans have to question me about my farming until I was able to tell him that I was shortly due at his High Commission in Trafalgar Square. "And why are you going there?" my new friend asked. "Well, I'm taking a bunch of farmers to your country to look at the agriculture and I am hoping someone there might be able to advise me what to see", I replied. "Maybe I can help", he said, "I happen to be the South African Minister of Agriculture", and pointing to his companion, "this is my Permanent Secretary, Mr Van de Meuwe".

Soon after that two elegant ladies arrived, who were introduced as the wives of the Minister and his Permanent Secretary. As our conversation continued it emerged that they had come over to make contact with our Agriculture Minister who happened to be John Gummer. But he had declined to see them, presumably because apartheid was still too fresh in the memory, and they were still persona non grata. Instead of seeing Gummer they had seen the late Baroness Jean Trumpington who was, at the time, agriculture spokesperson in the House of Lords. Knowing the lady, as I did, I felt sure she would have given them a few laughs. But they still felt let down at not being allowed to see the top man.

As the conversation continued, I let slip that I did a bit of broadcasting and wrote columns for a farming magazine and the *Financial Times*. The Minister, whose name was Krai van Neikerk, repeated that he would like to show me things that I would never see on my trip. "You can be my guest", he said, "Give me your card and I will write to you when I get back". Obviously I said thank you very much but continued hesitantly, "My wife will be with me". "That's OK, she can come too", he said, and the four of them went for lunch in the Club restaurant while I went off to the South African High Commission in Trafalgar Square.

Arriving home that night I told Lorna about the encounter with the South African Minister. But I don't suppose we'll hear any more from him, I said. That would be too good to be true. But three weeks later a letter arrived bearing a Pretoria postmark. The letter asked if I could let the Minister know where our study tour would end so that Lorna and I could be picked up. It went on to propose a ten-day tour of places we would not have seen on our study tour and said we would be accompanied by two top government advisors and one of their wives who would be company for Lorna.

And it all happened just as promised. At one point we drove across the Karoo, an area of desert populated only by scattered tiny Bushmen to the town of Uppington, where we went to a little agricultural show featuring mainly Persian fat tailed sheep and met the Minister and his wife. He was electioneering for the referendum on majority rule which took place just a few days later in March 1992. Lorna and I joined the Minister and his wife, Therese, in the back of his government Mercedes as we toured his constituency around the town. We went to house meetings and public meetings and then to Krai van Neikerk's farm a few miles away. He had 32,000 acres and the total stocking was 1,300 Merino ewes, which took us two hours to find. The average annual temperature we were told was over 40 degrees C, and average annual rainfall was 6 inches per year.

A few days later we went to a polling station to see how voting was going, and witnessed queues of Zulu and Khosa people voting for the first time, and having purple dye sprayed on their hands to stop them voting more than once. Our study tour had been really good, but the ten days spent in the privileged position as government guests were even more fantastic. I had never had such access to a minister before and we came away thinking we understood so much more about South Africa, its problems as well as its beauty. And it all began in the bar at The Farmers Club. I could go on about other influential people I have met there but it would seem like name dropping. Suffice to say it happens a lot.

One day, when I was in the Club in 2000, an old friend and past chairman of the Club, Norman Shaw, a northern Irish dairy farmer and much more, came up to me and said "David, why have you never been on the Club Committee?" I replied that it was probably because no-one had asked me. To which he said he was asking me now, and if he proposed my name would I stand? I replied that I would, and the next year was elected to help run the Club. I served two periods of three years, and then had a statutory year off wondering if I should allow my name to go forward again. But I had enjoyed the committee work so much that in spite of my advancing age I decided to stand. I was duly elected for two more three-year terms.

During those years I served on the Membership sub-Committee; the House sub Committee and the Journal and Communications sub Committee which I chaired for a few years. Such jobs take time and they cost money because committee members are charged for bedrooms just like every other member. But on the committee you are mixing with some of the most interesting people in the industry; you get to hear some of the best speakers at committee dinners; and the camaraderie of the Club is that much more intense. I have now retired to leave room for other, younger people to have their turn and bring their fresh ideas to the Club. But I regard my entire membership – now well over 50 years long – as an enhancing experience that has made my life, and that of Lorna, my wife, who joined me at the Club on countless occasions, so much more enjoyable. My years on the committee were an added privilege. And I thank all who served with me for their company and their friendship.

Chapter 27

Eastern Counties Newspapers

In the 1960's when I marched into the offices of the *East Anglian Farming World* and demanded to see the editor because he had omitted to send a reporter to my YFC meeting on the Common Market, the firm was headquartered in London Street in Norwich. It was a narrow street in the middle of the main shopping area and it's difficult to imagine it now, but buses used to go up and down it when I was young. Buses have, of course, got much bigger but even so I wouldn't want to try to drive even a small bus down it today. In fact I couldn't because London Street was one of the first in Britain to be pedestrianised, a status it still enjoys today.

Long before traffic was banished, Eastern Counties Newspapers, the owners of the farming paper together with daily, weekly and evening papers for both Norfolk and Suffolk plus a few magazines, had decided they should relocate to offices that were more accessible. They didn't move far – just to the end of the street. But that move only lasted a few years before they moved again to a much more prestigious purpose–built site overlooking Norwich Castle and the old cattle market which by then was being expensively converted into a shopping mall and underground car park.

I was working at Anglia TV offices in the old Agricultural Hall on the opposite end of the same cattle market site on a regular basis through the 1980's, and was fascinated to witness the extensive and longwinded archaeological excavations that took place before the shopping mall could be erected. All sorts of historic items were found, as might be expected from an area that had been the centre of trading in the city for hundreds of years.

By the end of the 1980's the shopping mall was finished and open, and Eastern Counties Newspapers offices and printing presses stood regally at the top of the hill with a view across it all, in a position fitting for a family owned company of such high local standing. Its history dates back about 150 years when three families, the Colman's, of mustard fame, the Tilletts who were Norwich jewellers, and the Copeman's, who had a background in journalism, decided to start a daily newspaper for Norfolk people. And although there have been many managers, editors and journalists over the years who were not from those families, they and their descendants were still the dominant shareholders – until recently. More on that later.

For the record, the company had other premises in Ipswich from which The *East Anglian Daily Times* was printed and published. But the Norwich building was where the senior management had their offices and where all the strategic decisions were made. The management structure was an overarching Group board which oversaw all the company's activities under which there was an Ipswich Executive board and a Norwich Executive board to decide on matters in their respective geographical areas. The Chairman of the Norwich board was a friend of mine of long standing, Geoffrey Copeman.

One day in 1990 he phoned me and invited me out to lunch. He wanted to discuss something with me, he said. It turned out there was a vacancy on his Norwich board and by the end of lunch he had asked me to fill it. He said he thought my pedigree as a Norfolk man born and bred and my experience in broadcasting and journalism both local and national would be an asset to the company. I was delighted and surprised to be given such an opportunity and accepted immediately. There followed a six year spell on that board, from which I derived a great deal of pleasure. I also learned a lot about the "other side" of journalism which is not always clear to people like me who had previously just provided copy for printing.

While I was on the ECN board we made a number of fundamental decisions about our publications. One was to change our flagship daily, the *Eastern Daily Press*, from a broadsheet format to tabloid – although we resisted calling it tabloid to try to avoid being compared with *the Mirror* and *the Sun*. The discussions about this change were long and sometimes quite tense. Some board members felt the small size would make it appear that we had dumbed down. Others, myself included, said the size of the pages did not dictate the quality of the news they contained; that provided our journalists maintained that quality, any suspicion that we were cheapening our paper should quickly be dispelled. But it took a long while for some doubters to be convinced.

In the event the conversion to tabloid went ahead, and although some readers agreed with the doubting board members at first, the change was soon accepted - and the content quality maintained. I suspect most readers appreciate the ease of handling the smaller paper as they scan it over breakfast and would not vote to return to a broadsheet. Similarly travellers on cramped trains to London and elsewhere would not find a broadsheet as easy to read as the smaller offering we launched in the early 1990's. A few years later The Times followed our example vindicating our decision.

Another fundamental debate while I was on the board was to build a new print centre in Norwich. Our existing presses were based on the traditional hot metal principles that had been used for years. They were expensive to run, and because of longstanding Fleet Street tradition, could only be operated by unionised labour. But new digital technology was being developed that would allow direct input of copy onto presses and produce better quality printing. These were difficult decisions and there were many aspects to consider.

The cost, which we estimated would be between £25m and £30m was only part of it, for to derive full benefit from the technology we would have to face the inevitability of making many people redundant and that in turn would cause problems with the print unions. To cut a long story short all of those issues came to the fore and had to be dealt with. Some were easier than others but eventually peace was restored and the project went ahead.

The next challenge was to make best use of our exciting new facility. And it wasn't long before news of its capabilities spread and we attracted significantly increased quantities of contract printing. Much heartache and head scratching had gone into that new print centre, but it turned out to be the right move for the company in the end and it was churning out countless papers and magazines.

At around the same time that I was involved with Eastern Counties Newspapers (which, incidentally, has adopted the new name, Archant, since I left the board) an opportunity presented itself to bid for a local radio franchise for Norfolk. I was invited to join a consortium to bid for the franchise and there followed a frantic round of strategy meetings under the chairmanship of Ian Mackintosh, a local man and chairman of the chocolate factory bearing his name. ECN was also involved in the bid.

We were advised that the broadcasting Authority in whose gift the franchise was, were looking for maximum community and geographical involvement in the management structure, and we were a very mixed bunch. I remember meeting Ian Mackintosh one evening in Norwich and asking him how he was getting on completing the group that would submit the bid. "It's going OK," he said, "but to complete the line-up I could really do with a black lady vicar from Lowestoft". Sadly, just before we were due to appear before the Authority, Ian collapsed and died of a massive heart attack. It was a tragedy for his family, of course, and probably scuppered our chances of securing the franchise. The winners were a group called Radio Broadland and they are still broadcasting today.

Recently Archant, ECN's new name, have decided to re-launch a farming magazine with the historic title *East Anglian Farming World*. It's not a weekly like the one I wrote a Young Farmers column for all those years ago but is published a few times a year, and funded by advertisements from farmers and crucially the ancillary trade. I have been invited to write a column in each issue. It has more than a touch of the déjà vu about it, and only a few ancient readers will remember my original involvement with the title. But I take pleasure from the opportunity to renew my involvement with a company with which I have enjoyed an amiable relationship for many years.

Sadly, however, Archant has fallen victim of the rush to online news. Its advertising revenue fell like a stone and although it managed to survive longer than most newspaper publishers in 2020 it had to call in administrators. All the titles were sold to new owners who have continued publishing daily newspapers (as well as the *East Anglian Farming World* for which I still write), and the uninformed would hardly know the difference from the traditional family ownership. But business casualties have become commonplace especially after Covid19, and we just have to get on with the changes.

Chapter 28

All Corners – the house that never was

As I passed the allotted life-span for man, "three score and ten" according to the Bible, I began to pressurise our landlord's agent to agree to allow my second son, Rob to inherit my Agriculture Holdings Act (AHA) tenancy of Whiterails Farm. Tenancy law stated that if a son or daughter spent most of their time working on a farm and derived most of their living from that activity they should be eligible to inherit a tenancy. This applied for three generations and I was the first, so Rob would be the second.

The fact that we owned other land, which it could be said occupied Rob for part of his time, and contributed to his income, were not grounds for stopping his accession, we were advised by our lawyers. In any case Whiterails was the centre of operations, so we saw no reason to delay the change-over. The landlords' agents obviously thought differently and negotiations dragged on. Eventually, after some years, we were advised that the only way to resolve the issue was for me to retire so that the future of the tenancy could be decided – in court if necessary.

At least my announcement of intended retirement provoked action, and at last we were able to argue our case. It turned out that our legal advice had been sound, and after further protracted negotiation it was agreed that Rob should inherit the tenancy. It wasn't just the land at stake. Over the years since I had taken the farm in 1958 we had built barns for grain storage, a continuous flow drier to condition the grain, a workshop, a machinery store and so on. In fact it was the hub of our arable activities and carrying on with the type of farming we had established would have been virtually impossible without these buildings.

When I was first a tenant we had used some of the traditional buildings to store grain in 16 stone and 18 stone sacks. Later, as we converted to bulk handling and storage, we had converted the old buildings for fattening pigs. Later still, once we had bought other land nearby, we built a specialist new complex for the pigs on land that we owned. The new buildings were properly insulated, unlike the old, converted ones, and were therefore more comfortable for the pigs, and more efficient for converting feed into meat.

Once the pigs had been relocated, we were left at Whiterails with the traditional buildings for which there was no modern farming use. They had small doors that would not allow access to tractors and even if they had, the roofs were too low for tractors to work. What, we wondered, could we do with them that was useful and profitable?

Then, one summer's day at the Royal Show at Stoneleigh, Rob and I met a farmer who came from near Heathrow Airport. It turned out that he had faced the same dilemma a few years previously and had converted his old buildings into stables. There was a keen demand around his farm for accommodation for riding horses, he told us, and it was quite a profitable enterprise.

Rob, who had been keen on horses all his life, asked the man if we could visit his stables for a look round. The answer was yes, and a few weeks later we found ourselves walking round dozens of stables with aircraft roaring overhead. We learned a lot that day, not least that the mainly lady horse owners could be very demanding. But on the journey home we visualised how our old buildings could be turned into a stable yard and by the time we arrived had made up our minds to have a go at a livery.

We started slowly with just a couple of horses owned by a pilot and his wife and gradually expanded as demand increased, converting pig pens into stables as required. Over time we added an all- weather manege, a horse walker, and other facilities demanded by our growing list of clients, and before we knew it we had established a useful diversification. As indicated it was based at the rented Whiterails Farm and we didn't want to lose the income it generated any more than we did the farm buildings.

The next problem was where Lorna and I would live once the transfer of the tenancy had been completed. Understandably the landlords insisted that Rob and his wife Liesl should live in the farmhouse in which Lorna and I had lived for over 50 years. We had discussed the matter many times over the years and had decided we would like to retire into a timber structure of the kind we had stayed in many times when we had skied in Switzerland and Austria. We both loved the smell of timber and knew that, properly insulated, such a dwelling would be warm, especially if we had a log fire in the centre of a big room.

We also knew exactly where we wanted to build it. In the corner of a meadow, facing due south and overlooking land that we owned. It would be behind high hedges and trees and yet only 70 yards from a road. It would be close to three other houses, two of them converted barns, and help complement the small community that already existed.

Only a few years earlier Lorna and I had been in Finland on one of our farm study tours, and our party had visited a manufacturer of sectional log houses that could be purpose made and imported into England ready to be erected on a prepared site. In truth, one of the reasons we had organised the visit because of our interest in the log houses produced there. When we got home we employed an architect to draw-up our vision based on what we had seen, of what we wanted, and made an appointment with the planning inspector at the local council.

I explained to him what we would like to build, and where and why, and showed him the maps and carefully drawn plans. "If I were you, Mr Richardson", he said, "I'd go home and forget it". Shocked, I asked him why. "You can't build in open country", he told me. But it's not, I protested, it's tucked in the corner of a field close to three other houses and completely screened by hedges and trees. "By my definition its open country," he replied, "and you haven't got a hope of building where you want to."

But I am really keen on this site, I told him. So, if you were me what would you do? "I've told you already", he said, "I'd go away and forget it. But if you insist on trying to bend the rules I suppose you could sweetheart members of the planning committee – I don't doubt you know some of them – and try to persuade them to back you against me. But if you do you will have made an enemy of me and I will do my best to stop you. "

He went on, "You could, I suppose, bring me plans for some contemporary mansion with architectural merit that we would have to take seriously, but I doubt if you want to spend that much. Or you could come forward with an idea to build a structure with some novel local material that might appeal to the planning committee. Like straw, perhaps." And with that he rose from the table and returned to his ivory tower.

Needless to say I was taken aback by such curt treatment and I was discussing it with Caroline Drummond, who I had appointed to run LEAF many years before. "Don't discount straw," she said, "a friend of mine is building with straw as we speak. Maybe he can help".

A couple of phone calls later and I found myself talking to Craig

White, who I subsequently found out was an expert on designing with straw. He invited us to go to the University of Bath where his firm had erected a show house made of straw bales. Lorna and I loved it as soon as we walked into it. It felt warm because of the insulating properties of straw, and the plaster that had been rendered onto the straw had a really solid look and feel about it.

It was explained to us that were we to opt for such a dwelling we would be able to use straw from our own fields; that the bales could be built into prefabricated panels in our own barn; that some of our own farm labour could be used to help with this; that once constructed, the panels would be plastered on both sides and left to cure for a few weeks before being transported the short distance to the site where they would be erected, again using our own farm labour and forklift tractor. The roof could also be made of straw bales supported by a frame, and we could have solar panels on top.

There would be no need for a fire of any sort because the structure would be insulated to what was internationally known as "Passivhaus" standards, and if any warmth were needed on bitterly cold days it could be provided by underfloor heating powered by the solar panels.

I commissioned Craig White to design a house incorporating all the elements we required – a single story structure with a large reception room - come dining room - come kitchen in the centre; two en-suite bedrooms at one end and a utility room, an office and a garage at the other. The whole structure was to look like a Norfolk barn from the outside, and was to face south, overlooking our land. I planned to run a few cattle or sheep on the meadow in front of the big picture window so suggested a ha ha beyond a small lawn so that we had an unrestricted view of the animals and our land and crops behind them.

We commissioned an energy survey which stated that if built, it would be one of the most energy efficient structures in the country. With solar panels on the roof it would produce more energy than it used, including cooking, washing, cleaning, etc. We also commissioned an environmental survey which revealed that although there was a pond a hundred yards away there were no natterjack toads or other rare animals that might inhibit or delay the building, nor were there any bats nearby.

Once again I presented plans to the local planning officer and a date was fixed for them to be considered. I wrote an email to all the members of the planning committee explaining in brief what I had in mind and why it was necessary. I mentioned that my wife was now registered disabled and that level floors rather than steps were essential. And I referred to the novel building material – straw – that would be so local it would come from the field adjacent to the site.

I went to the meeting and some of the councillors said they were concerned at the scale of the plans, which I'm sure they had misunderstood, and turned it down. Their decision was also undoubtedly influenced by the negative advice of the planning officer who once again stressed that the plans called for building in "open country". They appeared to be unaware of, or ignored, all the positive things like energy efficiency and local labour and materials, or the fact that the neighbours had actively welcomed the project and there were no public objections.

But the week after this refusal Eric Pickles, the Local Government Minister stood up in the Commons and said he wished local councils to take a more relaxed view of planning applications to help solve the shortage of houses in rural areas. I rang the planning office and asked if this meant conditions for acceptance had changed. The officer said they might have and agreed to allow my proposal to go before the committee again. Another date was set for the hearing and we put the proposition to the planning committee again. This time Craig White an acknowledged world expert on straw buildings helped argue the case. He pointed out that if erected this would be the most advanced dwelling of its kind in the country and would attract people from miles around to come and see it.

The chairman of the Committee, Joe Mooney, an Irishman who settled in England many years ago, said he thought this was the kind of ground-breaking development the committee should allow, and said he would be voting for it. He then opened the matter up for debate. The first councillor who spoke said he noticed there was a ha ha on the plans. The only people he knew who had ha ha's, he said, were stately home landowners who wanted to pretend they owned even more land than they did.

A second councillor said that he noticed the face of the ha ha was to be of local stone." But we don't have local stone in Norfolk", he concluded. Had he looked out of the window of the Council chamber he would have seen flints scattered across most arable fields. Stone age men made axe heads with them, and they have been used as building materials for thousands of years. That is what was meant, but I was not allowed to correct him.

A third councillor said he noted that I had a wife who was disabled and couldn't get around very well. "If I had a wife like that," he said, "I wouldn't build a house in open countryside, I'd buy a bungalow near a bus stop." None of these so-called objections had anything to do with planning law, of course. All they did was to expose the prejudices of the Councillors. And with that the matter was put to the vote. And we lost again.

I still didn't give up. I went to appeal and some weeks later an appeals officer came to inspect the site. The planning officer arrived too and accompanied us. "What a lovely spot," said the appeals officer, I can see why you want to build here". He stayed about ten minutes then off he went with the local planning officer in tow. Three weeks later he too, turned us down.

Finally, I went to see my MP, a Conservative, at one of his surgeries. I showed him the plans and the artists impressions and he said the proposed dwelling looked really lovely. "So what do you want me to do?", he asked. I told him I wanted him to take the case to Eric Pickles and ask him to overturn the local result. Oh, I'm not sure I can do that, he replied. South Norfolk is a Conservative Council and I wouldn't want to get wrong with my friends there.

That whole process, from conception to final rejection took three years and quite a lot of money spent on architects and surveyor's fees for plans that were ultimately aborted. I was certain we had a just case and would win. We even had a name for the new dwelling – the same as the field in the corner of which we wanted to build – All Corners. But there comes a time when you can't fight officialdom anymore and I had reached that point.

I remain angry and disgusted at the way we were treated and my faith in local democracy has been irrevocably destroyed, not least as I see even now as I write, the first of over 1,000 houses being built in a village less than two miles south of here and more than 2,000 in a small town a mile to the west. I just needed permission to build one environmentally friendly house on my own land, which only those wanting to come and see me would have known was there.

Clearly we had to think again and the obvious solution was to swap houses with Rob and Liesl. They had bought a former farmhouse from my brother and I when they married, and had spent a lot of money modernising and extending it. It is bigger than the retirement home we had hoped to build and has two stories rather than being on one level. We had to install a stair lift for Lorna, and converted a normal bathroom into a wet room for her. Sadly she is no longer here to use either.

It's a nice comfortable house and we settled in very happily, which, after 54 years in Whiterails, took a few months. It has the added attraction of being close to where we wanted to build the straw house so we can still enjoy some of the same sunsets that we had been looking forward to. But it isn't what we wanted and it doesn't allow us to continue what Norfolk is famous for: "doing different" to benefit the environment which the straw house would have done.

Chapter 29

The run up to the millennium

When our father died about 400 acres of tenanted land was lost to the surviving partners, my brother Philip and I. It was land that had been specifically let to him, and its owners wanted it back to farm in hand. Although this was not unexpected it was a bit of a blow. We had done a few other land purchase deals over the years, mainly surrounding the main block at Gt Melton, and had geared the operation to run 1,400 acres. Over the next year or two after father died we managed to replace some of the acres we had lost but most of the new land we acquired was six or seven miles from the main steading so was nothing like as convenient as that which had been next door.

Meanwhile my second son Rob had come back from a gap year in Australia keen to start a sheep enterprise. He bought a few hundred ewes to start with and ran them on the limited acreage of grass we had available. But to make his business viable he became a contract shepherd and took on the management of other farmers flocks. He also bought a mobile dip which he towed behind his truck to treat flocks all over Norfolk. In the season he joined others in a shearing gang, and again travelled around the County to provide a shearing service. In addition as his numbers grew he rented grass keep for them from a number of farmers within reasonable distance of home. Even so he had to spend a lot of time driving from one flock to another and Lorna, and me to a lesser extent, were often called in to check all was well with some off-lying flock.

As we progressed through the 1980's political and economic pressures intensified. As already discussed public pressure on contemporary farming methods was increasing. This in turn meant government was less sympathetic to farming of all kinds. We were running three pig enterprises – the biggest one based on the main block of land in the new piggeries we had erected plus two smaller ones on small farms we had purchased in buildings that were less efficient and more difficult to manage. As profits declined we decided to rationalise down to just the biggest herd and sell the other two. To compensate for the loss of income we decided to become a multiplication herd for the Pig Improvement

Company (PIC). This meant buying superior breeding stock from PIC and breeding them to produce females for onward sale through PIC to commercial pig producers.

The concept was sound in that we could expect premium prices for the stock we produced and therefore better profits than we would get for pigs sold for pork and bacon. And for a while it seemed to work as planned. But the pigs we bought from the parent company came from a variety of sources and each source had its own set of health problems. Before we knew it our herd had all manner of diseases, none of which were serious on their own but collectively became very troublesome indeed.

Our previous policy had been to keep a closed herd and only bring in the occasional boar, or male pig, for breeding purposes, which would be isolated from the rest of the herd until acclimatised to the bugs in our buildings. That way we had few health problems. But this new system that was supposed to enable our herd to be healthier than ever turned out to have the opposite effect. In the end we decided we had to sell out of all pigs, steam clean and disinfect the buildings, leave them empty for several weeks, and then re-stock with clean, disease free, pigs from one source. It was an expensive operation, obviously leaving us with a big gap in our income, so was not undertaken lightly. But it seemed to be the only solution.

Meanwhile, Philip became increasingly involved in pig politics, being elected to serve on a number of industry bodies. He had an analytical brain that few farmers possess and was able to interpret increasingly complicated legislation coming out of Brussels for other members of these specialist bodies. This resulted some years later in him being presented with The David Black Award, the most prestigious in the pig world, for services to the UK pig industry.

Arable farming was under pressure too and surplus production continued. To limit the amount of arable commodities produced the EU decided to introduce set-aside – an idea originated in America which stated the percentage of each farm that must be left uncropped, or set-aside, each year. For farmers who had been farming during and just after the 2nd World War, when they had been urged to produce as much of every commodity as they could, this was an anachronism. But they had little alternative but to comply with the ruling in order to sell what they produced on the rest of their holdings.

190

Soon after that, environmental restrictions were introduced that required farmers to create habitats for birds by planting wild bird mixtures of seeds along field boundaries, protect the quality of water in ponds and ditches, only cut hedges every three years and so on. Some farmers were incensed at such restrictions and declared they would carry on as they had always done. They claimed, with some justification in many cases that they looked after their farm's environment already. Although they meant they provided habitats for pheasants and partridges to shoot, there is no doubt that habitats created for game birds benefit many other species as well. But their arguments did not go down well with some conservation organisations which had much more benign ambitions to protect all birds and not just game.

Watching all this from both sides of the fence, so to speak, as a farmer who shot occasionally, and as a person working in the media where opinions are very different, I could see an urgent need for something to be done to bring the two sides together; to try to bring about some understanding of the farmers viewpoint among consumers and at the same time trying to soften aggressive farmers attitudes to "ignorant townies". It was these feelings that prompted me to write columns in *Big Farm Weekly* promoting such ideas and which subsequently led to the invitation to speak in America, after which LEAF was born.

There was no dramatic improvement in farm fortunes in 1990's, except when Britain came out of the Exchange Rate Mechanism, which gave us a boost – not because of good crops or good weather, but because of the rate of exchange between Britain and Europe, and our exports became cheaper and more attractive overseas. But that was a one off not to be repeated. On the farm, Rob had become disillusioned with sheep because prices for lamb were so low, and had eventually sold out of that business and come back home to join the arable crew. To replace that activity he had started offering horse livery services using the old pig buildings – an enterprise that was to grow as years passed.

Anglia TV's management decided that *Farming Diary* was no longer viable or necessary. The Programme Controller was heard to say that "with all the grain mountains around there was no longer any justification for a programme that taught farmers how to grow more wheat." He had clearly not watched the programme for years because we were not doing the type of programmes he alleged, nor had we for ages. We were, in fact, reflecting environment concerns of the kind I have discussed above and were very contemporary in our programme material. You could just as easily have said there was no longer any justification for the News.

Such arguments were put in hundreds of letters written by irate viewers who did not want to lose the weekly farming programme. Some were written by VIP's, MP's, and local government officers, but all to no avail. The programme came off the air in the autumn of 1991 and I suddenly had more time back on the farm.

At around the same time The *Financial Times* got in touch to say they too felt food and farming was no longer a live issue with all the surpluses around and had decided to devote the space on the Commodities page, which I had been filling every Tuesday, to heavy metals. The Editor there was obviously responding to the same perceptions that had persuaded Anglia to drop *Farming Diary*. My off-farm income declined as a result of these two decisions but I had had a good run. My TV "career" had originally, in 1960, been set to run for six weeks, and all my radio and writing invitations had sprung from that. So I could hardly complain.

Farming rumbled on through the 1990's with my brother and Rob and I, now released from some of my outside activities, working more closely together. Then one day Philip came into the office and said he would like to start running the business down. He was ten years younger than me but was clearly becoming disillusioned about farming and wanted to take life a bit easier. More to the point his two children were not interested in farming. His daughter was a speech therapist and his son was an architect, so why should he continue to work hard if they did not want to take over part of the business when he retired?

This created a dilemma for me because my son Rob was keen to try to build the farm up, given a chance. How could we resolve it? We discussed possibilities for months but whatever I came up with did not suit Philip and what he suggested did not suit Rob and I. Eventually, as has happened with so many farming businesses in similar circumstances, the only solution was to split the business. Philip offered to take the pigs, and Rob and I said we were content to take on the arable. Fortunately both elements of the business had similar turnovers and the house locations in which we both lived fitted as well. And so, the partnership we had built up over so many years split in half and some of the economies of scale were lost.

Over the next few years pigs were a dead loss and Philip had a hard time, eventually selling the pig unit and retiring completely. Arable farming wasn't too bad for the first year or two after the split but soon followed pigs into the doldrums. The years since the millennium have been unexciting for most UK farming businesses apart from the occasional brief highlight caused by temporary world shortages and there have been times when I wished we had sold the whole business instead of splitting it. But that would not have gone down with the next generation on my side of the family so that was not seriously considered.

Towards the end of the 1990's Rob's elder brother, Andrew, telephoned from America to say that after eighteen years living and working over there he had decided to come back to Britain. He had moved on from managing land under irrigation through a few other jobs away from farming and had ended up specialising in the American coffee industry. He had been watching the progress of Starbucks, the Seattle based coffee bar chain, and thought it might be a good time to try to develop something similar (but smaller) in Britain.

Costa, the Whitbread subsidiary, had already come to the same conclusion, plus a few smaller companies, but with his industry experience across the USA, Andrew reasoned this merely confirmed his view that coffee bars represented an opportunity in the UK that was ripe for exploiting. He began searching for locations, and wrote a franchise manual for those who might want to join him, and pretty soon he and associates had opened eight coffee bars across the country.

One of the biggest problems he encountered was securing good locations with high footfall. As a small, start-up Company he did not have the financial record or credibility of Starbucks or Costa, or indeed of the many mobile phone companies that were looking for multiple city-centre locations at the time. There was, in the early 2000's a retail boom, and property owners were demanding huge, premiums and in many cases uneconomic rents for good sites. He was chasing around the country wearing himself out trying to help his franchisees and not making a big enough margin to justify the effort.

It was while he was worrying about this that Nestlé's offered him a job running their subsidiary company, Nespresso, managing their coffee capsule business in the UK and Ireland. It was too good an offer to turn down and he wound down his franchises and took it. For a few years he built up capsule and coffee machine sales across the UK and several international markets for Nespresso, until he was offered an international position building coffee bars around the world by Whittard's which had just been taken over by Icelandic entrepreneurs. Coffee bars were his first love so he took the job and all went well for a while, until the Icelandic financial bubble burst. Chaos ensued and Andrew, along with many others, was out of a job just as the recession was beginning to bite.

It was a difficult time for him and he had little option but to offer his coffee expertise as a consultant. And then his situation got even worse.

He received a message from a police officer in Acle in East Norfolk not far from Gt Yarmouth. Would he please call in at the police station there next time he was passing. From the tone of the message Andrew assumed he may have been caught speeding or some other minor offence, and a few weeks later dropped in to see the officer.

The policeman sat Andrew down in his office and asked, "Do you own a pistol?" And although Andrew had forgotten all about it he was forced to agree that, yes, he did.

Years before when he had been farm managing in Texas, one of the hazards he faced on a daily basis was rattle snakes. On several occasions he had disturbed nests of snakes when he had been out soil sampling and a couple of times he'd almost been bitten in the leg; once he was bitten by a rattler, but luckily was wearing boots – like most US farmers and cowboys who wear the high leather boots, to protect against snake bites. He had told his boss about this and his reaction was "Well, just shoot the critters". Andrew replied that he hadn't got a gun to which his boss said, "I'll give you one". And for the rest of his time as a farm manager in Texas and Nebraska, he kept the revolver in his truck but only ever used it, on snakes, a few times.

As his jobs changed the gun was put in a shoebox and kept in a cupboard in which ever house he was living in. And when, may years later, he and his wife and daughter decided to move back to England Andrew contracted with a removals firm to ship their goods across the Atlantic. He organised three piles – one to come to England, one to be delivered to his wife's father's farm in North Dakota, and one to be thrown into a skip. Sadly, the removal men were not very reliable. Some of the things that should have come to England, like his wife's wedding dress for instance, never arrived and has never been seen since. And other things, like US electrical appliances, not compatible in the UK, and the pistol in its shoebox, which should have been sent to North Dakota, arrived in England.

When he found it under lots of clothes Andrew knew he shouldn't have it in England and would have to dispose of it. But he was working hard to launch a new business and it slipped his mind. It was left at the bottom of the box in which it arrived and sometime later when space in the UK house where the family was living was at a premium, the box and all its contents were taken to a storage firm for safe keeping. He'd have been better to have disposed of the lot at the time but did not have time to sort it out so took the quickest option. Then, to make matters worse, he had been travelling in America and elsewhere for weeks at a time supervising the building of coffee bars for Whittards when an invoice had arrived from the storage company. The invoice had somehow been mislaid and when the storage company had not been paid they simply sent the contents of the storage unit – including the shoebox – to an Acle auctioneer to sell. The auctioneers had found the pistol in the shoebox it had been put into some 26 years earlier, and reported it to the local police.

Andrew explained all this to the policeman who was very understanding and relaxed about it. "Don't worry too much," he said," we will have to send the case to Court and you'll probably get a few hours community service." A judgement that was confirmed by a probation officer who called to see Andrew a few weeks later.

Needless to say Andrew was embarrassed by the whole affair and said nothing to the rest of the family hoping the judgements he'd been given would go relatively unnoticed and that he would be able to deal with whatever punishment he received as quietly as possible. He had pleaded guilty and had not bothered retaining a solicitor. Clearly he was being naive but he had lived under US law for eighteen years where every second housewife carries a gun in her handbag.

So, when he stood in the dock at Norwich Crown Court he was completely unprepared when the judge sentenced him to five years in prison. Indeed he was so shocked that he collapsed and had to be carried from the court. And the first Lorna and I knew about it was a phone call to say Andrew was in Norwich prison.

You can imagine how we felt. It was as if a bomb had dropped on our family. The following day the case took up the whole of the front page of the *Eastern Daily Press* and although I was not involved, apart from being Andrew's father, I was interviewed on local TV. I explained that Andrew was not a criminal and that forensics had determined the revolver had not been implicated in any crime; that he had not used it for any purpose other than killing rattle snakes many years before in a country where such things were quite legal; and that I thought a law that locked a person up for five years for forgetting something was an ass. But the fact remained that his sentence was the recognised tariff for owning a firearm in the UK without a licence.

Lorna and I received hundreds of letters of sympathy, as did Andrew in his prison cell. Many friends offered to try and help and I accepted advice from a number of those who were familiar with the law. We went to appeal with the benefit of a barrister speaking for him and at the second hearing the sentence was reduced to three years, which was better, but still an appalling prospect for Andrew. We decided to appeal again to the High Court at the Old Bailey but there was a delay of several months before the hearing.

Meanwhile Andrew's health began to deteriorate. He had by this time been transferred to Wayland Prison near Thetford where he suffered a series of black-outs. He was taken by ambulance to the Norfolk & Norwich hospital where he was diagnosed with severe heart problems. From there he was sent to Papworth hospital near Cambridge where he underwent a quadruple heart bypass. In passing it is worth noting that apart from when he was on the operating table he was at all times being guarded by two prison officers, one of whom was permanently handcuffed to him.

He came through the operation OK, and the time for the High Court Appeal drew nearer. At our suggestion, the barrister speaking for Andrew contacted the heart surgeon to ask if he thought Andrew's sentence had anything to do with his heart problems. The surgeon replied that the shock and stress of the sentence had almost certainly been the root of the problem. He pointed out that it was unusual for a healthy man of just over fifty to have such a serious condition. This was evidence the barrister would later use at the appeal.

I attended the court at the Old Bailey on the appointed day. Three judges sat together to hear the evidence having reviewed the facts of the case beforehand. As they delivered their judgement it soon became clear that they thought a miscarriage of justice had taken place. The burden of what they said meant that Andrew would be released immediately. I leaned forward and tapped the barrister on the shoulder and whispered, "Ask for costs". He did so, and costs were granted without argument.

That gesture alone implied that they believed Andrew to be almost innocent apart from his forgetfulness.

And so, eight months after he had been sent to prison Andrew walked free. But the experience took much longer than that out of his life, and he had undergone life threatening surgery in the middle of it. Today, after a slow start after his release, he has re-established himself as a successful coffee consultant advising people around the world. He started, and is CEO of a couple of international companies developing high-profile speciality coffees, and encapsulating them into bio-degradable capsules for use in the millions of coffee machines in circulation, thus maintaining the family tradition of supporting small farmers (in his case throughout the coffee growing world) and caring for the environment.

He is also a trustee of a couple of charities, one to help young people stay on the straight and narrow and away from drugs and the other to promote UK produced food to UK consumers. Andrew wrote a small book while incarcerated on his observations of prison life and what he thought should be done to reduce re-offending. This was reviewed by influential people and copies went all the way to the Home Office. But friends who lived through the experience with our family still greet me by asking "how is that son of yours who went to prison?" They don't forget. And neither do we.

Chapter 30
Discussion paper 2007

By about 2005 it was becoming clear to me that the agriculture policies being broadly followed were increasingly inappropriate. Ministers and EU officials were still relying on outdated ideas of reducing production, while it was becoming obvious that the industry needed to concentrate on how to increase the amount of food available to consumers. And this was not just of concern to Britain but the whole world.

I was picking up information from the internet and elsewhere about the near certainty that the world's population would rise to over 9 billion within the foreseeable future, and what this would mean to demand for food. And I was painfully aware that productivity increases on farms had stalled. No longer were we seeing the dramatic jumps in crop yields that we had seen in the 1970's and 80's. And political actions, and in some cases, inaction was to blame. Furthermore the politicians with whom I came into contact seemed oblivious to what was happening, and Britain's self-sufficiency was beginning to decline.

Margaret Beckett had been appointed Secretary of State at DEFRA in 2001 and much of the blame for this attitude could be laid at her door. She spoke at the Oxford Farming Conference one January, spouting the usual platitudes we had come to expect from her, and a questioner from the floor had the temerity to ask, what was her food policy? She didn't answer the question as is so often the case with politicians, so at the press conference after her speech I put it to her again – had she even got a policy for food? I asked, and had she ever asked her civil servants to assess what production policies we needed in the UK for the future, as the number of mouths increased?

She looked across the room at me with eyes blazing, clearly very angry at my impertinence. "I would not dream of wasting my civil servants time on such matters", she replied through gritted teeth. "The world is awash with food", she went on, "and we can import any amount from other countries, cheaper than you can produce it here. There is no food self-sufficiency crisis, nor will there be. So stop wasting my time by pretending otherwise".

Mrs Beckett was moved from DEFRA in 2006, but in the five years she had been there, the culture she had created had put back farm progress much more than that. She was wrong and I knew it. So, in 2007 I wrote a discussion paper entitled *The Challenges Facing World Agriculture* and distributed it via email to all my contacts. Some of them forwarded copies to their contacts, and the paper must have been read by several thousand people. *Farmers Weekly* then published an extended summary which about 75,000 buyers of the magazine might have read – or, if *Farmers Weekly's* claim that each copy is read three times on average is true then many more will have seen it.

Whether my thoughts made any difference to official thinking I cannot say. But a couple of years later the Government Chief Scientist, Sir John Beddington, together with dozens of his eminent colleagues around the world, published a report which said virtually the same as I had, even using some of the same statistics to make their point. I take the liberty of repeating here an edited version of what I wrote in 2007. As you read it please remember it was published at least a couple of years ahead of the governments approved version, and even further ahead of several similar reports that have been published since. I have inserted a few contemporary updates in square brackets.

THE CHALLENGES FACING WORLD AGRICULTURE

and the implications for policy makers

by David Richardson OBE FRAgS

SUMMARY

To feed a population that will grow from 6.3billion to 9.5billion over the next forty years it will be necessary to:
double the total production of food.
triple crop yields per hectare.
and do it on less land with much less water.

INTRODUCTION

Fifty years ago food was rationed across Europe and farmers were urged to produce more. Forty years later they had been so successful that there were lakes of milk, mountains of grain and more. Limits were imposed on production and land was compulsorily left idle.

Today, following a dramatic rise in world population; increases in demand from fast developing nations; the diversion of significant volumes of farm commodities into biofuel; the preservation of land for specific environmental purposes; and changes in the world's climate, we once again face the prospect of food shortages.

This discussion paper is intended to help increase understanding of the implications of these changes, suggest measures the author believes should urgently be adopted and promote debate that recognises the vital importance of production agriculture.

DEMOGRAPHIC TRENDS

It is widely accepted that the population of the world stands at some 6.5billion and that this will increase to 9.5 to 10.0billion by 2050. The increases will be greater in developing countries than developed countries. The two leaders in population growth, according to the World Bank, are China (currently 1.3billion) and India (currently 1.07billion). Economic growth in both has been dramatic in recent years and as incomes have increased demand for more and better food has followed. In India, for instance, it has been shown that where incomes have risen from $1/day to $2/day expenditure on food has more than doubled. In China, where similar income increases have occurred, food expenditure has tripled. The same pattern has been observed throughout the developing world.

These trends are set to continue. Further, rising populations will be increasingly urban. More people will become consumers instead of producers of food. They will settle around existing cities and towns taking up land that previously produced crops for consumption. Most cities were originally established in areas of good land so, by definition, more of it will be lost from food production creating greater demands on other areas where the land may be of lower quality and production potential.

It has been calculated (by the World Bank) because of higher populations and increases in individual income and demand, that world food demand will double by 2050. But land depletion around cities and the fact that there is only about 12% of land left in the world that has yet to be cultivated (assuming the Brazilian rain forest, the world's biggest carbon sink, remains substantially intact) means that yields per hectare will need to triple to satisfy the anticipated demand for food.

BIOFUELS

It should be noted that the above takes no account of the current trend, in many countries, to use farm produced commodities as feedstocks for biofuels in response to the run-down in supply and high price of fossil fuels. Moreover, the diversion of some 70million tonnes of US maize to ethanol production rather than export for food this year has exacerbated the world feed grain shortage and had a significant impact on raising world grain prices. In Britain, the spot price of grain is approximately twice as high as this time last year creating severe problems for livestock farmers reliant on bought in grain-based feeds for their rations.

Other farm produced feed stocks are also being used for biofuels. Oil seed rape from the western world and palm oil from countries like Indonesia for the production of biodiesel; sugar and wheat for ethanol; and the burning of fibre crops such as cereal straw, miscanthus, willow coppice and forestry waste to generate electricity. Predictably there is a great deal of enthusiasm for these developments from farmers. They see them as providing additional markets for what they produce and creating sufficient demand to maintain current market prices. For their costs for energy, fertilisers, pesticides, and indeed most other inputs required for crop production have risen rapidly recently.

Sadly, few of these energy sources are truly sustainable, for two reasons; firstly because the energy derived from the processes is often little more than the energy that has to be used to extract it; and secondly because most biofuels require government subsidies to be viable. In countries where subsidies are generous, such as the USA and Germany, the development of biofuels has been swift and dramatic. In other countries where subsidies are much smaller, such as the UK, progress has been much slower. Without substantial aid even crude oil prices close to $100/barrel are insufficient to encourage widespread investment in bio-fuel alternatives. Given the expected future demand for food the wisdom or otherwise of building up a subsidy-based biofuel industry is much debated.

INHIBITORS TO PRODUCTION

It has been estimated (by WWF International) that some 67% of the World's fresh water is used for agriculture. As populations increase and prosperity spreads demand for water will increase. But because of these developments, availability per person will be at least one third lower than it is now. There will be shortages and in the battle of priorities agriculture will almost certainly lose. As an American farmer who had lost his water rights in Colorado told me many years ago, "Them folks in Denver changed the laws of nature. They made water run uphill – towards money". The same will be true around the world and farmers who currently rely on water to help them grow their crops will have to find ways to do without.

[In Norfolk where I live farmers who irrigate are now, in 2021, enduring a similar experience to those in Colorado. The authorities have decided they need more water in London and the home counties and have notified the farmers that their water abstraction licences are to be reduced and in some cases removed. So, water that would otherwise be used to produce soft fruit or vegetables or potatoes will now be piped south to flush toilets in the suburbs of London]

It is too early to be sure what effects Climate Change will have on farm production in the medium and long term. All we know is that there have been aberrations in the weather in many areas of the world in recent years. There have been droughts in large areas of Australia that have decimated grain harvests and caused sheep and cattle to be shot because there was no grass for them to eat. In the mid-west of America slightly less serious droughts have reduced the production of wheat and soya beans for the last two years. There have been ultra-cold winters in the Ukraine and Russia that have killed off autumn sown wheat. And as we know well, there have been intermittent droughts and floods across Europe as average temperatures have risen.

Whether these phenomena have been because of natural variation in the weather or something more sinister is open to argument. But there is no doubt they have caused massive problems for farmers and made the production of commodities a great deal more difficult. If global warming continues and by definition, becomes more severe, farming systems will have to change. In the meantime production will suffer from extremes of weather.

THE GLOBAL CHALLENGE

To summarise – the farmers of the world will need, over the next forty years, to double the total production of food; to triple yields per hectare; and to do it on less land using much less water.

The Rev. Thomas Malthus said just over two hundred years ago (1798) that the World would run out of food. We didn't, and he's been something of a laughing-stock since. But could his predictions be about to come true at last?

Certainly to avoid that happening the world needs to take the possibility (some say probability) seriously and take action now. Why the urgency while Tesco's shelves are full? Because it takes ten years to develop a new variety of seed and bring it into commercial production. And the huge increases in production and yield that are called for cannot be achieved in one giant leap. It will take a long period of sustained research and application and a number of steps to respond to the scale of the challenge. As one of the world's top plant scientists said to me recently – "there are possibilities of meeting the challenges ahead but research budgets have been slashed and are currently inadequate to tackle the scale of the problem."

It should, by now, be clear that the production of sufficient food for the future poses a dilemma that is at least equal in importance and urgency as that of dealing with Climate Change. Furthermore, that the two are inescapably linked and that production agriculture can, by raising output and reducing the movement of bulky commodities around the world, be part of the solution. But while a great deal of political capital is being invested in climate change there is little parallel debate on the provision of food.

SOME OF THE ANSWERS?

A massive worldwide research effort needs to be undertaken to establish how to grow crops in changing climates that yield better and are more nutritious. In addition scientists could intensify their search for crops that are tolerant to drought. While doing so they need to identify strains that are resistant to diseases and viruses, that can thrive without pesticides and which have enhanced shelf life to reduce waste. Those involved in research into livestock farming need to look for the animal equivalents, especially with regard to diseases, for the most intractable of which they should create vaccines.

At present the majority of such research is entrusted to multi-national concerns whose research is often limited to the most potentially profitable innovations and/or concentrated on exploiting other products of their company. I am not suggesting their work is of no value. The reverse is clearly true in most cases, but to balance their commercial interests and to ensure substantial research is devoted to the public good there needs to be a significant build-up of state funded, independent research with centres all around the world co-operating, even more than at present, to maximise international progress. Given the inevitable time delays in getting results from such work it is urgent this starts now.

GMO's

Much of the research envisaged will centre around variations on genetic modification. I am, of course, aware that despite the fact that British scientists are among the world leaders in the technology, this remains controversial in the UK. There appears, however, to be greater acceptance of it and some relaxation of the regulations surrounding it in Europe. Spain was allowed to grow 75,000 hectares of GM maize last year, for instance, with lesser areas in Portugal, France, the Czech Republic and even Germany, to deal with serious problems with corn borers. As yet, no commercial GM crops of any kind have been grown in the UK.

Some 100million hectares of GM crops were grown around the world last year with no ill effects on the people who consumed them. This area has increased from a standing start about ten years ago making it the fastest world-wide adoption of a new agricultural technology ever known. If Britain continues to resist the adoption of good science we will be denying our farmers the opportunity to compete on world markets and even more importantly, contributing to a shortage of food that might be avoided. At present we have a policy that is part science and part public opinion. That public opinion is led by hostile single issue pressure groups. It is hardly surprising policies are inconsistent and illogical.

[Since I wrote those words the area of GM crops grown around the world has increased exponentially. And still no ill effects have been reported. And still there are no GM crops grown for human consumption in the UK although, since Brexit, Defra and the Prime Minister, Boris Johnson, have expressed themselves supportive of a variation of the technology. This is Gene Editing which should be less controversial than Genetic Modification. For whereas GM may involve mixing the genes from different species, which is what critics call "playing God", gene editing is what it says on the tin – the editing or slightly changing the genes within a species. Moreover it is the technique used to develop Covid vaccines. I hope this fact becomes widely appreciated and that this might help to persuade people to accept gene edited food]

WHERE ARE WE NOW?

UK and EU policies have been equally inappropriate in other areas of land use in recent years. They have concentrated almost entirely on enhancing the environment while assuming that food security was not an issue. Phrases like "the world is awash with food for us to import", have been commonplace and retailers have been encouraged to scour the world for cheapest possible supplies. Warnings that this would lead to a run-down in domestic production have been ignored.

Suddenly there is not as much food out there as was thought. In any event it is costing much more than it did. The cost of food, that has risen slower than most other prices for the last fifty years and has therefore been deflationary, has suddenly shot up and is in danger of becoming inflationary. The Prime Minister *[Gordon Brown at the time]* has suddenly realised there may be a problem and has initiated an enquiry into whether food security matters.

But he has left it rather late. Since 1995 Britain's self-sufficiency in foods that can be produced at home has reduced from 86% to an estimated 70%. The food trade gap – that is the trade deficit between the food we import and that which we export - increased from £6bill to more than £15bill in 2005 so it is probably nearer £20bill now. A downward spiral of that magnitude gathers momentum and is difficult to reverse. The gap will almost certainly grow bigger before it can begin to recover – if, as I fervently hope, that is what the PM's enquiry suggests should be attempted. However, it is extremely doubtful that officials and ministers at DEFRA, who have demonstrated little understanding of the industry over which they preside, have any idea how to set about rebuilding production.

[Gordon Brown's enquiry did, indeed, call for more self-sufficiency and said most of the right things but my predictions that the situation would get worse before it got better have sadly been confirmed. Self-sufficiency has now gone down to nearer 60% and the food trade gap is about £26billion. Figures which I suggest spell imminent crisis. But still the Trade Department of government resist the concept of keeping out any imports of food that do not comply with the standards in force here. Yes, they have appointed a Commission to advise on imports but have reserved the right to ignore that advice, thereby keeping the right to import what they like at any price. The NFU has pointed out that this endangers the viability of domestic production to which the Trade Department shrugs its shoulders and essentially says - so what?]

RE-ESTABLISH PRODUCTION EXPERTISE AND ADVICE

I will not attempt here to specify all the measures that need to be taken to re-build production and re-establish farmer confidence in government except to say that chief among them will be the adoption of policies that are practical and achievable.

But one key element in tackling the task would be to re-establish regional advisory committees composed of leading practical farmers and advisors who understand what would be required and what it would take to motivate farmers and researchers. Combined with an immediate injection of cash for research and some inspired advice at farm level, appropriate policies might begin to get a response from the industry within a few years. Issuing edicts on top of regulations wrapped up in red tape will not achieve such a response.

CONCLUSION

It would not be much of an exaggeration to suggest that within the foreseeable future it will be necessary to deal with the production of food as during a war.

Many deep thinkers have come to the view that DEFRA in its current structure is an inappropriate department to deal with the challenges this paper has outlined.

The management of this huge task will require a government department dedicated to food production.

Such a department should be created, populated, and advised by people who actually understand agriculture and the food industry and why sustainable growth in food production is a prime responsibility of government and farmers together.

Caring wildlife conservation and environmental management can be balanced alongside and integrated with the priority of food production.

The writer was, in 1991, the founder chairman of LEAF (Linking Environment And Farming). The balance between production and care for the countryside was one of the main objectives we espoused then and have promoted and practiced since. LEAF principles could be applied across the whole of agriculture alongside the necessary increase in food production. It is a proven virtuous circle.

In the end the judgement of future generations will depend on whether we accept the inevitability of change and plan for it with foresight so that we survive and leave our successors a viable world. Or whether, by inertia and misguided policies, we allow ourselves and our children to become its victims.

[November 2007

Bear in mind when that paper was written. And consider what has happened since. Most dramatic has been the comparatively recent exit from the EU with all its unintended consequences to trade with Europe. We left with a deal. Whatever would it have been like without a deal?

But when it comes to domestic food policy the situation has got much worse. Led by the nose by misguided economists and single-issue pressure groups the government has pursued a policy that puts the environment ahead of everything neglecting the production of food.

Don't get me wrong. I am an environmentalist, as I hope this book has illustrated. But I fervently believe food can and should be produced in harmony with nature, and that it is possible to achieve optimum production while enhancing the environment. We will fail our customers and consumers around the world if we do not do so.]

Chapter 31

Conclusion

It is several years since I wrote and distributed that discussion paper. And I was just one of the first to point out problems that other, cleverer people than me, have repeated ad nauseam ever since.

To be fair some politicians have begun to pay lip service to the message, but little has been done to address the issues and the Covid19 pandemic has inevitably delayed things further. The Coalition government under David Cameron found £160million for basic research and that was noteworthy and potentially helpful, as was the introduction of AgriTech East in Cambridge under the directorship of Dr Belinda Clarke, which is intended to help fill that gap and is a template for what is needed across the country. But the interpretation and application of research work nationwide has been like a huge vacuum since the government's free advisory service, ADAS, was virtually wound up thirty or forty years ago. And in any case, as discussed in the previous, chapter the ruling culture is one of giving priority to green issues rather than production. This in turn delays, if not stops, the introduction of new technology, and inhibits increases in production.

When I wrote in 2007 that action was needed NOW, I meant it. The ten-year lead time that it takes for most agricultural innovations to be taken up and put into use commercially still exists, and the first ten-year period is over. I wonder how much longer it will take for politicians to wake up to the growing urgency for action. Sadly, short termism rules, and the only priority for some politicians is gaining or re-gaining power.

Meanwhile agriculture in the UK is being left behind the rest of the world. I said in my discussion paper that in 2007 an estimated 100 million hectares world-wide were growing GM crops. As I write that figure has far exceeded 200 million hectares. And yet not a single hectare of UK grown GM crop has been allowed to be harvested for human consumption. Those plots that have been planted at UK research establishments where Britain is a world leader in developing the technology have all been destroyed on EU and UK government instructions. The ridiculous thing is that many of the processed foods and ingredients for animal feed that we import into this country and consume every day have been made with GM produced commodities grown in other countries where cultivating them is legal. And I would not mind betting, if I were a betting man, that the pants you are wearing as you read this are made of GM cotton. But still modern-day Luddite's reject it as dangerous, clearly without understanding what they are saying.

European farmers, and that still includes the UK even out of the EU, are the victims of single-issue pressure groups and the *Daily Mail*. That, of course, is too simplistic but The *Daily Mail* slavishly prints and supports every unscientific utterance by Green Peace, Friends of the Earth, the Soil Association, and others that allege horrendous consequences should we produce GM or GE crops in the UK. So why are those consequences not being experienced in the scores of countries where such warnings have been discounted?

I do not claim, and nor do the scientists who have developed the technologies, that they are the answer to all our problems, and can solve all the future food production demands of our expanding population. But what they can do is contribute to those solutions and enable farmers to grow crops that are drought resistant, able to absorb nitrogen from the air, are potentially beneficial to human health, and with fewer chemicals. Whether or not those crops yield bigger tonnages, and experience shows that some do, the reduction in chemical use is surely worthwhile in itself.

I mentioned in the discussion paper how grain prices had suddenly peaked to provide the occasional profit boost for growers. This was because of temporary shortages on world markets, and some would say gave credibility to the policy of allowing market forces to rule. But in the years since the millennium there have been only two or three years when farmers have made respectable profits from staple commodities. The rest have been at best break even, with losses recorded on all but the very best land. But you cannot run an efficient business when you only make decent profits one year in about three or four. You cannot invest in the latest technology, and thus your efficiency suffers. This, in my view, is one of the main reasons the yields of many crops have plateaued and not increased in line with varietal improvement.

This in turn has resulted in many farmers exiting the industry with their land being taken over by others. If the trend continues small farmers will disappear, and we shall be left with a few big farming companies.

Yes, I know I was part of Sentry, but for the most part the company is managing for small and medium sized farmers in order to help them stay part of the industry. So, I would deny that my opinion contradicts my position.

Indeed one of the positive things I am doing in my dotage is to try to help young people with limited resources – like me when I started – to get a foothold in the farming industry. My old friend Henry – Lord – Plumb invited me and a half a dozen or so other friends to help him set up a Foundation in his name to provide some funding for young people, and even more importantly, to allocate them a mentor to advise and hold their hand while they get started.

I was thrilled when Henry asked me to be a trustee of his Foundation, and as I write we've been operational for about six years. Like me, Henry left school without many qualifications, to help his father when his workers were called away to the 2nd World War. Like me, Henry joined a Young Farmers Club, and although it was informal, acquired an unofficial mentor to guide him. I owe a huge debt of gratitude to my own informal mentors, and although my achievements are dwarfed by Henry's, I was pleased to be given the opportunity to share my good fortune and put something back into the farming industry that has given me so much.

Well over a hundred candidates have already been helped, and we have high hopes for most of them. It would be wonderful if we succeeded in identifying other potential male or female "Henry Plumb's" to go on through their lives to serve agriculture as he has done. To continue the initiative we need to raise more funds so that the charity can continue indefinitely. For we are going to need many more motivated young people in future to produce food for the growing UK and world population. The Henry Plumb Foundation is doing its bit to try to ensure they are there when we need them.

In the foreseeable future (see my forecasts in the last chapter) I believe, along with those who seem obsessed with buying farms at any price at the moment, that the demand for what farmers produce will far exceed the supply. Market forces may then be the right policy, although I fear politicians will want to control the worst excesses that could occur, as their pet policy of today leads to exorbitant food prices. But that's for the future. Meanwhile I strongly believe that measures should be introduced to level out the volatility of recent years and provide a degree of stability.

If that does not happen, the farming industry will haemorrhage even more skilled workers and small farmers so that when they are desperately needed to maximise production in a few years they will not be there.

In America they have a system of counter-cyclical aid. It works inversely to the market in that when production of a commodity is seen to be rising its price is reduced; and when production is seen to be falling the price is raised. It's more complicated than that, of course, and needs a lot more detail to make it work. But a system like that could help stem the tide out of agriculture and I believe that is important.

And there are precedents in this country. As I pointed out earlier when Fred Peart was Minister of Agriculture and pigs were having a particularly difficult time, he introduced just such a scheme and it transformed the fortunes of farmers with pigs. And so far as I can remember it took fewer civil servants to administer it than exist today in DEFRA. The difference is that in those days they felt they were there to help farmers produce food, whereas today they seem to want to hinder.

The fact is I have lived long enough to see and experience many policies towards farming. I've experienced rationing and had my own ration book, out of which my school tuck-shop lady cut a coupon whenever I bought a bag of toffees. I've seen surpluses and their political consequences when land had to be taken out of production to avoid making the situation worse. And I've seen history repeating itself as I feel sure it will again. But politicians and their advisors have short memories and usually fail to learn the lessons of history.

And as many nations of the world descend into chaos in disputes over territory and religion – which will have been exacerbated by Covid19 - I hope that wisdom and experience will prevail. As a young child I remember a World War even though I was only two years old when it broke out and eight when it ended. Those memories are still vivid despite my youth at the time. As we recovered from that conflict, our way of life gradually improved and, with a few hiccups, has continued to get better every year since. But as I look at my grandchildren who are blissfully unaware of what is going on in the Middle East and the virtual renewal of the Cold War in Russia and elsewhere, I wonder what the future holds for them.

Needless to say I hope they have as happy a life as I have been blessed with. But still I worry, and wonder, and pray.

I cannot end this narrative without paying tribute to my late wife,

Lorna, who has passed on since I wrote the original version. For 59 years she encouraged and supported me. When I was away she replaced me and constantly kept an eye on the farm. And also when I was away she was both mother and father to our family.

But she didn't stop there. When the Women's Farming Union was initiated nationally, she started a branch in Norfolk, and chaired it for several years. Under her leadership it thrived and I was pleased to support her and attend some of her meetings. She was devastated when the national organisation was wound up, largely as a result of infighting among some of its members.

Lorna was also the driving force in the publishing of a pocket booklet entitled "Love it Eat it" which was one of the first to explain and promote the benefits of local food. That booklet is still in print and being distributed by LEAF as part of its educational initiative.

Many years ago when I was still a Young Farmer, I arrived home from a Council meeting in London and told her someone had written some verses for a Young Farmers song based on the motto "Good farmers, Good Citizens, Good Countrymen" and that a tune was needed. That evening she sat in front of our piano and composed one and it was sung at every main YFC event for years. For Lorna was a skilled musician and I loved hearing her play. I miss her very much.

Lightning Source UK Ltd.
Milton Keynes UK
UKHW020629080621
385137UK00004B/267